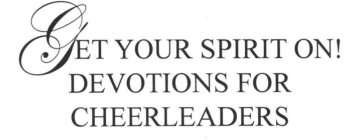

GET YOUR SPIRIT ON! DEVOTIONS FOR CHEERLEADERS

By
MICHELLE MEDLOCK ADAMS

SonRise Devotionals
Lighthouse Publishing of the Carolinas

GET YOUR SPIRIT ON! by MICHELLE MEDLOCK ADAMS
Published by SonRise Devotionals, an imprint of
Lighthouse Publishing of the Carolinas
2333 Barton Oaks Dr., Raleigh, NC, 27614

ISBN: 978-1-946016-28-7
Copyright © 2018 by Michelle Medlock Adams
Cover design by Elaina Lee - forthemusedesigns@gmail.com
Interior design by AtriTeX Technologies P Ltd
Cover photo courtesy of Jeff Richardson, Richardson Studio Ltd., Bloomington, IN.

Available in print from your local bookstore, online, or from the publisher at:
www.lpcbooks.com

For more information on this book and the author visit:
www.michellemedlockadams.com

Brought to you by the creative team at Lighthouse Publishing of the Carolinas
(LPCBooks.com): Amberlyn Dwinnell, Eddie Jones, Shonda Savage, and Cindy Sproles .

Library of Congress Cataloging-in-Publication Data
Adams, Michelle Medlock
Get Your Spirit On!/Michelle Adams 1st ed.

Printed in the United States of America

"This inspirational, uplifting devotional will keep girls on the path of positivity. Cheerleading offers opportunities to shine God's light, while teaching young girls discipline, strength, sacrifice, and gratitude; all the more reason to get your spirit on!"

- Hannah Carrico, Former Indianapolis
Colts Cheerleader and Chicago Bulls Dancer

"Michelle Medlock Adams captures the heart of cheerleading in her devotional *Get Your Spirit On!*. I love how she intertwines her passion for Jesus with the skills and vocabulary of cheerleading. She reminds us that God is our ultimate cheerleader in this life and through prayer, journaling, and knowing His Word we can grow closer to our Father. As a former coach of elementary cheerleaders and a current coach of high school cheerleaders, this is a devotional I would recommend for any age cheerleader."

- Lori Cummings, Bedford (IN) North Lawrence
High School Varsity Cheer Coach

"Michelle Medlock Adams has written an essential devotional for cheerleaders! Every page of "Get Your Spirit On," will be an inspiration to face difficult days and situations with determination, dignity and a Christlike perspective. Thanks to her cheerleading experience and expertise, along with her desire to equip her readers with a stronger faith, she has written a devotional that will "fire up" all cheerleaders to use their gifts for God's glory!"

- Gwen Thielges, author of the college
athlete devotional, "All In For Him."

Table of Contents

For my two favorite cheerleaders,
Abby Leigh and Allyson Michelle.
Love you both more than you'll ever know.

Foreword

*A*t my first high school pep rally, I sat in the bleachers with my one upperclassmen friend—my only friend at the school actually—a little overwhelmed with all of the noise, excitement, and rowdiness that comes from getting out of class forty-five minutes early. When the cheerleaders performed a dance in the middle of the gym floor, I hit my friend in the arm.

"I'm going to be a cheerleader," I said. I couldn't stop watching them. They all looked so pretty and confident—everything I wanted to be.

My friend laughed. The thought of shy, unpopular, bookworm Bethany as a cheerleader was hilarious, apparently.

"Yeah right," he said.

I didn't care. I knew I would wear that uniform one day, and every girl would want to be me, and every guy would want to date me.

That last part didn't necessarily work out, but I tried out for the basketball cheerleading squad a few short months later. Seeing my name on that list made me sob in the school parking lot, and my mom said she prayed the whole time I walked from the car to the white sheet of paper taped to the gym doors.

Cheerleading was my escape from being "the Jesus girl that nobody really knows."

It was elite.

It was competitive.

It was perfect, and it was mine.

I can't even imagine how much fun Michelle Medlock Adams and I would have had if we'd been on the same cheer squad. I know that we'd have become instant friends, just like we did in real life.

The first time we met, I was walking down the hallway at a conference when this blonde whirlwind rushed past me. She looked stunning in her black ensemble, perfect makeup, and hair expertly curled.

"I *LOVE* your belt," I said as I spun on my heel. She stopped mid-step, pivoted to face me, and her eyes lit up, and she smiled.

I imagine that's the same face the crowd saw when she yelled for her school's team to beat 'em, knock 'em, rock 'em, sock 'em.

"Thank you!" she said, and she was gone.

I sat in her workshop later that day, and then we ended up chatting for over an hour after her class. We connected on so many levels, and funnily enough, not only had we both cheered through high school, but we were also coaches.

Although it's not every little girl's dream to coach cheerleading, it was one of mine. Cheer gave me confidence and brought me out of my shell. To be the Assistant Coach for a State Championship squad brought that experience full circle—Go Knights!

The fire, strength, and passion you need to get through hours of a football game on your feet under the bright hot field lights (#CheerIsASport) is the same determination, spunk, and resilience Michelle carries with her today. She is a force to be reckoned with, able to dig deep inside of herself and give everything she has with a smile on her face. Not only is she a bestselling and award-winning author and speaker, Michelle keeps her athleticism alive by taking five-mile hikes, bass fishing, and teaching fitness classes at her local gym.

Michelle's book *Get Your Spirit On* brought all the wonderful memories of high school flooding back. Because cheerleading gives you one of the top social platforms in the school, you get to be a great example of how cool kids can love God. Never forget that the majority of the kids in your school think you're popular, even if you don't feel like you're in the top circles.

As a writer, my advice is to buy a journal that you love and use it for the *Ready. OK* times.

As a mom, my advice is to make memories—as many *Toe Touch Moments* as you possibly can. When you read through the devotionals, make a point to follow Michelle's *Jump into Action* suggestions.

As a cheer coach, my advice is to stretch every day and cheer from your diaphragm, not your throat, so you don't get hoarse. And bases, lift with your legs. That's where your power is. Flyers, aka "top girls," squeeze your tushie together. It'll make you feel lighter. Back spots, you're the key and the glue. If the flyer falls, she lands on you. Every. Time. You rock. In honor of our best back spot ever, #CarsonSavesLives.

As a former cheerleader, my advice is to breathe in every moment while you're in uniform. Don't take it for granted. Use your platform to be kind, a good student, and a leader, because somewhere in the stands at your next pep rally is a shy insecure girl who wants to be just like you.

Blessings and Brilliance,

Bethany Jett
Award-Winning Author, Speaker,
Former Toe-Touch Master (almost)

Introduction

I pushed through the crowd of other pony-tailed girls for a glimpse at ... the list. It had been four hours since freshman cheerleading tryouts, and now was the moment of truth. Having cheered in sixth, seventh, and eighth grades, cheerleading had become a big part of my life, and I wasn't ready for that part of my life to end. My heart was pounding so hard I was sure others could hear it.

Out of the 64 girls vying for six spots on the Bedford North Lawrence High School Freshman Cheer Team, had I made it? My eyes scanned each number—*where's 23?* I looked down at the number on my chest, just to make sure it didn't match any of the six numbers on the list, but I already knew the answer. I hadn't made the squad. I felt like I'd been run over by a huge truck and then backed over. I congratulated the girls in the corner who were already celebrating their accomplishment of making the squad, which included my very best friend in the whole world, and then I walked out the gym door.

I couldn't believe I'd have to sit on the sidelines that year—it's a place I'd never been before. Of course, I was sad and disappointed, but the fact that I hadn't made freshman cheerleader didn't diminish my love for the sport. I tried out for the high school dance team called "The Starsteppers" a few weeks later, and I made that squad. We performed at halftime of all the football and basketball games, and I enjoyed it very much. But, my first love was always cheerleading. So, I worked hard on my gymnastics skills to prepare for future cheer try-outs. I had intended to try out for the JV squad the end of my freshman year, but I didn't. I was doing well on the dance team and was even named a co-captain my sophomore year, so I continued dancing right through my junior year.

As March of my junior year rolled around, my best friend Angie, who had been on the BNL cheer team since her freshman year, stopped at my locker one afternoon and said, "You HAVE to try out for cheerleader this year ... we have to cheer together our senior year."

"I have no shot of making it now," I answered. "I haven't cheered in three years! That's a lifetime in cheer years!"

She wouldn't give up. Day after day, Angie encouraged me to try out.

I wanted to try out—more than anything—but fear of failure was holding me back. I kept replaying in my mind the day I looked at the list of freshman cheerleaders and found that my name wasn't on it. I wasn't sure I could go through that again.

Still, I practiced my round off back handspring series in Angie's front yard, and she taught me the motions to the school song, just in case I found the courage to try out for the Varsity squad later that month.

A few weeks later, I joined over 70 girls in the gym for cheer tryouts, and at the end of the week, I did my best to "wow" the judges. I wanted to cheer Varsity that year and make more cheer memories with my bestie, but I had already made peace with the fact that it wasn't likely I could beat out the girls who had made it every year in high school.

That year, my name WAS on "the list"—I made the BNL Varsity Cheer Squad along with five other girls. It was the best year ever! Our squad qualified and competed in Cheer Nationals in Orlando, Florida, that year! And, our boys' basketball team went all the way to the State Championship tournament at Market Square Arena in Indianapolis, Indiana. So much fun!

I share both of those experiences with you because I want you to know that as I wrote these devotionals

for you, I have been on both sides of "the cheer coin."
I've been that girl who didn't make it, and I've been the
girl who made the Varsity squad against all odds. I've
sat in the bleachers during games and hollered from
the stands, and I've cheered my heart out alongside my
fellow cheerleaders from the sidelines.

I went on to cheer in college, married my high
school sweetheart, and we had two little cheerleaders
of our own. Both of my girls cheered—on All-Star
teams and school teams. In fact, my oldest daughter,
Abby, went on to cheer in college and even received a
cheerleading scholarship. Abby and I then partnered
together to coach cheerleading in our hometown. And,
we've also judged cheer tryouts throughout the community. Plus, as a writer, I've written for "American
Cheerleader" "American Cheerleader Jr." and "Cheer
Biz" over the course of my journalistic career. So, you
might say I've been around the cheer world most of my
life, and in that time, I've seen the good, the bad, and
the ugly. But, I'm happy to report that I've seen a lot
more good than bad, and a lot more pretty than ugly.

Let me share just one example of what I'm talking
about. When Abby and I coached the Shawswick Elementary cheerleaders a few years ago, we had worked
hard to prepare our new squad for the BNL Cheer
Clinic and Competition, and they had performed well.
We had quite a bit of talent on our seven-member

squad, so we were also expecting to win several awards. As the music began, and the BNL cheerleaders fired up the elementary cheerleaders, coaches, and parents who had just arrived for the awards presentation, I whispered to Abby, "I just hope that all of our girls get something—a spirit award—something." She nodded in agreement.

After all of the hoopla and grandstanding, our squad won an award for most creative home cheer, as well as a spirit stick for exuding school spirit. Also, three of our seven cheerleaders won individual awards—Kennedy won a best jumper award; Ally won a spirit ribbon, and Chelsea earned a best gymnast medal. As we took pictures of our girls with their group awards and individual merits, I noticed one of our fourth graders, Trista, wasn't as "spirited" at usual. In fact, she seemed quite depressed. I was just about to ask her what was wrong, when Chelsea, one of our individual award winners and a fifth-grade squad member, put her arm around Trista's shoulder and asked, "What's wrong?"

"I just wish I could've won an award," Trista said, with big tears in her eyes.

Without missing a beat, Chelsea handed Trista the "Best Gymnast" award and said, "You can have this one. I have others at home because I compete with an All Star squad."

Trista hesitated, not sure if she should accept it, but Chelsea insisted.

"Go ahead," she urged. "It's yours."

Trista hugged Chelsea and then literally bounced away like Tigger from Winnie the Pooh to show her mom the award, and I stood there in amazement at the selfless act I'd just witnessed. At that moment, I so wished I'd had an extra-special award to give Chelsea for her kind heart.

I'm not sure if anyone else saw what Chelsea did that afternoon, but I saw, and it inspired me. Later, I told Chelsea how proud I was of her, and she smiled and sort of brushed it off, not wanting me to make a big deal of it. But it was a big deal. Though Chelsea thought it was just a small gesture, it put a big smile on Trista's face, and it made a big impression on me. Coaches love that kind of stuff!

And, so does God.

That's the kind of heart and persona that I want all cheerleaders to be known for—not the catty, back-biting, shallow bubbleheads that are often portrayed in movies and on social media. We are so much more than that! You are so much more than that! Because cheerleaders have gotten a bad reputation in some circles, it's time we start living what our name declares we are—cheer-leaders! You know, the word "cheerleader" actually has the word "leader" in it, and that's no coincidence. Because as a cheerleader, you not only "lead" cheers, you are also a leader in your school and your community. Many cheerleaders go on to become great leaders in the world. (In fact, you'll read in the pages of this book about several who have gone on to be United States Presidents!) As leaders, cheerleaders are often observed and looked up to, which gives us a great platform to let the love of God shine big in us and through us. We need to take full advantage of that platform and start living what we believe. As a Christian cheerleader, you are the perfect person to lead others to Christ. What a privilege! Are you excited?

I wrote this book especially for you—to help you grow in your faith and to encourage you to lead others to God through your powerful witness. I guess you might say that I am *your* cheerleader, and I am honored to fulfill that role.

About this book ... You can do these devotions alone, during your own quiet time with God. Or, if your school and coach are OK with it, you can do these devotions with your fellow cheerleaders before practice or after, during "cheer bonding time."

Each day's devotion plays on the "cheering" theme, featuring special sections such as: Bible verses called "Strength Training", discussion questions called "Fire up!", a daily declaration called "Shout it Out!", a prayer called "Megaphone to Master", a journaling section called "Ready. OK.", and an application section called "Jump Into Action". I've also included a "Fit Tip" for

each day, and a new cheer or chant that you can teach
your squad. Yay!

It's a 40-day journey to a closer relationship with
God …

Ready?

OK.

Let's do this …

1

Rejoice in the Lord always. I will say it again: Rejoice!

Philippians 4:4 NIV

"Finding the Toe Touch Moments"

*Y*ou just passed your math test! The cutest boy in your whole class asked you to the school dance! Your cheer squad just made it to Nationals! You find out your family is going to Hawaii for Spring Break!

What do all of these things have in common?

They are "toe touch moments."

These are the times in your life when you'll want to throw the perfect toe touch out of pure excitement. These are times to celebrate, right? But, what about those not-so-toe-touchy moments? What about the times when you fail your math test? The cutest boy in the whole class asks your best friend to the dance. Your cheer squad doesn't qualify for Nationals. And, your family doesn't have the money to go anywhere for Spring Break this year. Ugh! Can you still keep a positive attitude during the less than toe-touchy times in life?

The Bible says that we should rejoice in the Lord at all times—good and bad. As difficult as that may be, we need to have a heart of praise even when the circumstances aren't so great. Plus, if you take a moment to think about all of the good things in your life, you won't be able to keep your praise inside! So, go ahead. Throw that toe touch in spite of the bad stuff going on around you. Praise the Lord all the time. If you'll praise Him in the less than toe-touchy moments, God will honor you.

STRENGTH TRAINING: Memorize James 1:2 that says, *Consider it pure joy, my brothers, whenever you face trials of many kinds* (NIV).

FIRE UP!: Do you keep a positive attitude when life isn't so "toe touchy?" Or, do you let what's going on around you determine your happiness?

MEGAPHONE TO MASTER: "God, help me to let my joy level be based on Your love and promises—not my circumstances. Thank You for all of the toe touch moments in my life right now and for all of the ones to come. I love You. Amen."

GIVE A SHOUT!: Say out loud: "I will rejoice in every situation."

READY. OK: Grab your journal. Think about the last week's not-so-toe-touchy moments … and write about the one that was the most difficult. Now, write the word "REJOICE" right over the top of that situation in big RED letters!

JUMP INTO ACTION: You know what takes your mind off of the not-so-toe-touchy moments in your life? Helping your friends get through their tough times. So, take a moment to reach out with God's love this week. If your friend is going through some difficult situations, be her cheerleader. Encourage her in every way.

FAST FACT:

Did you know that there are currently 1.2 million cheerleaders ages 6-11 in the United States and another 1.6 million ages 12-17?

FIT TIP:

Want strong abs? Of course you do! So, sit on a fitness ball with your feet shoulder-width apart. Now, place your arms across your chest (like you're doing a sit-up). Lean back until you feel your abs tighten. Hold for three to five seconds and then slowly and smoothly return to your starting position. Do this 10 to 12 times each night!

Here's a new cheer to try with your squad ...

Prepare For the Fight!

The Panthers are here! (x) Prepare for the fight!
We're back, and we're better!
In the silver, blue, and white! (x)
Get up! Get ready!
We'll show you how it's done!
The Broadview Panthers (clap, clap) are Number One!

*(x) = pause

*Put your school's colors in place of silver, blue, and white and your school's name and mascot in place of Broadview Panthers ...

2

*David was greatly distressed, for the men spoke of
stoning him because the souls of them all were bitterly
grieved, each man for his sons and daughters. But David
encouraged and strengthened himself in the Lord his God.*

1 Samuel 30:6 AMP

"Cheering Up Yourself"

Ever had a really bad day? I mean a really, really bad day.

A guy in the Bible named David had one of those bad days. He and his men were out fighting the bad guys, following God's orders, and when they returned home from battle, their really bad day began. As they approached their camp, they could see smoke.

When they finally arrived on the scene, everything was burned, and their wives and children were gone. Their other enemies had burned their belongings and taken their families captive.

Ugh.

The Bible says that David and his men cried until they had no more tears. Now that's a lot of crying! Then, David's day got even worse. His men were so upset that they started blaming David. They said, "This is all *your* fault, David!" and they threatened to kill him!

So, guess what David did? He cheered himself up. The Bible says he went off by himself and encouraged himself in the Lord. In other words, he reminded himself of all the good things that God had done for him and his family. He became his own cheerleader, encouraging himself right out of that depressed state and into victory. He reclaimed his belongings and his family. Then, just 72 hours later, he was made king!

So, the next time you're having a really, really bad day—don't give up. Follow David's example and encourage yourself in the Lord. Just think ... you might be 72 hours from your greatest moment!

STRENGTH TRAINING: Read all of First Samuel Chapter 30.

FIRE UP!: Do you encourage yourself in the Lord when you're in the middle of a really bad day?

MEGAPHONE TO MASTER: "God, please help me to turn to You when I need encouragement. Help me to remember all of the times You've come through for me in the past. Amen."

GIVE A SHOUT!: "God has come through for me before and He will do it again."

READY. OK: Grab your journal. Write down a few of the times God has come through for you. Now, take a moment to praise Him for those victories and get excited! He will do it again!

JUMP INTO ACTION: Why not start keeping a small praise notebook in your cheer backpack? Every time God does something for you—no matter how small or big—write it down. That way, you can use those times to encourage yourself in the Lord the next time you face a really bad day.

FAST FACT:

Did you know that 83 percent of all high school cheerleaders carry a B average or above?

FIT TIP:

Want to work on those obliques? Lie on your side on the floor in the same position you'd be if you were going to do a leg lift. Now, put the fitness ball between your legs and slowly raise your legs and the ball. Hold for three to five seconds and lower slowly to the floor.

Here's a new cheer to try with your squad …

Fired Up!

We're fired up! We're sizzlin'!
We're turning up the heat.
We're focused (clap) determined.
Our team can't be beat!

So come on crowd yell with us (x)
Yell: "Red, white, and blue!"
The OMS Stars (x)
are coming after you!

*(x) = pause

*Put your school's colors in place of red, white, and blue and your school's name and mascot in place of OMS Stars …

3

The human body has many parts, but the many parts make up one whole body. So it is with the body of Christ.

1 Corinthians 12:12 NLT

"Playing Your Part"

Mounts.

Whether you're a base or a flyer or a spotter, you have a very important part to play, and if you don't do your job, someone else will suffer. The flyer has to keep her body tight and hit her position with skill and control, or the whole mount will fall. The bases have to steadily lift the flyer and keep her secure, or the mount will be unstable and collapse. And, the spotters have to be right there in case the mount does fall. The spotters are crucial to preventing injuries.

Every single cheerleader has a part to play in order for a mount to succeed. And, the mount won't work well if the flyer suddenly tries to become a base or one of the bases decides to become the flyer. Each person has to play her specific role, or the mount will fail and ultimately fall.

It's the same way in the body of Christ. Each one of us has a special part to play in the Kingdom of God. You may be called to the mission field in Romania, or maybe you're called to write praise and worship music, or maybe you're called to start a prayer group that meets after school. Whatever God is calling you to do, go for it! Don't try to fill someone else's role—focus on your own! And, perform your role the very best you can.

Just think … if you're called to write worship music, one of your songs might touch the hearts of millions, causing them to turn to God. Or, if God calls you to the mission field, you might be the only person who will reach a certain part of the world with His love. So, be excited! You have a special part to play in this world, and God wants to help you fulfill it.

STRENGTH TRAINING: Memorize Jeremiah 29:11. It's a great "life verse." In fact, it's my favorite. *"For I know the plans I have for you," declares the Lord, "plans to prosper you and not to harm you, plans to give you hope and a future."*

FIRE UP!: Are you happy with your job on your cheer squad? Or, do you really want to be the flyer or another position instead? Why not be content with your own role?

MEGAPHONE TO MASTER: "God, please help me to be content with my role on the cheer squad and in life. And, please help me to fulfill both with excellence. I love You, Amen."

GIVE A SHOUT!: "I will fulfill the plans that God has for my life."

READY. OK: Grab your journal. Write down some of the plans you think God has for your life. If you aren't sure, ask God to show you. He will! Just pray and ask Him.

JUMP INTO ACTION: Buy a pack of white T-shirts and have a T-shirt making party with your cheer squad. Ask each girl to choose her favorite color of puff paint and then write her name on the front of the shirt and "Jeremiah 29:11 … Fulfilling God's plan for my life one day at a time!" on the back. These will make cute sleep shirts or maybe even matching camp shirts or practice T's.

FAST FACT:

Did you know that 80 percent of all schools in America have cheerleaders?

FIT TIP:

Warm up those legs! Start with your feet together. Now, step your left foot out and go down into a lunge. Next, place your right hand down by your left foot and lift your left arm up toward the ceiling. From here, switch legs as your move down the gym floor. You should feel a stretch in your legs, back and even shoulder area.

Here's a new cheer to try with your squad …

Number One!

Number One, we're back again!
Lincoln (x) Middle School is here to (xx) win!
Always on top is where we'll be!
The red, black, and white (x) the best, you'll see! (x)
Yeah! (x)
Panthers!

*(x) = pause

*Put your school's name in place of Lincoln Middle School and your school's colors in place of red, black, and white and your school's mascot in place of Panthers…

4

*So encourage each other and build each other up, just as
you are already doing.*

1 Thessalonians 5:11 NLT

"Be the Best
Benchwarmer!"

When I was in elementary school, I played on a
basketball team at the Girls Club. Well, I didn't actually play that often. In fact, I was more of what you might
call "a benchwarmer." I occasionally got to play at the
end of the game if we were WAY ahead. But, that was
OK. I didn't mind warming the bench because I knew
the other players were better than me. They'd play, and
I'd cheer them onto victory.

As it turned out, I made a much better cheerleader
than I did a basketball player. So, I tried out for sixth-

grade cheerleader, and I made it! Yay! But, you know what? I learned a lot from my bench-warming days. I learned how to be patient. I learned how to encourage others. And, I learned how to be content with the person God made me to be.

I truly believe if I had become bitter toward my teammates and my basketball coach, I would've never had the opportunity to become a cheerleader. God had to teach me some important lessons before I was ready to move off the bench and in front of the crowd. If you're a benchwarmer right now, don't be bitter. Be the best benchwarmer you can be! Keep your heart right, and watch God promote you!

STRENGTH TRAINING: Read First Corinthians Chapter 13 and see how to walk in love. Verse five tells us that *Love is not self-seeking*. But, we benchwarmers already knew that, right? ☺

FIRE UP!: If you're a benchwarmer right now, is your heart right? Or, are you bitter and jealous?

MEGAPHONE TO MASTER: "God, help me to make the most of my bench-warming days. Help me to grow and learn during this time so that I'll be ready when You're ready to promote me! Amen."

GIVE A SHOUT!: Say out loud: "I will be the best benchwarmer I can be until it's time for me to shine."

READY. OK: It's journal time. If you're on the JV squad right now, and you've been dreaming about the day you'll make varsity—tell God. Write a note to God and share your dreams with Him.

JUMP INTO ACTION: OK, so maybe you're on the B cheer team, and you'd much rather be on the A team. Don't be discouraged! Instead, write a note of encouragement to your fellow cheerleaders and your coach. Or, ask your coach if you can bring a special treat to practice next week for all of the girls. Find ways to motivate those around you.

FAST FACT:

Did you know that Actress Sandra Bullock was once a high school cheerleader?

FIT TIP:

To make your toe touches higher, sit on the floor in a straddle position and point your toes. Now, lift your legs off the ground and hold for three seconds. Do this eight times. As you get stronger, try holding your legs up even longer!

Here's a new cheer to try with your squad ...

We're Here to Win!

SMS Hornets are here once again.
Striving for excellence
We're here to win!
The purple, gold, and white (xx)
Let's win, tonight! (x)
Hornets!

*(x) = pause

*Put your school's letters in place of SMS and your school's colors in place of purple, gold, and white and your school's mascot in place of Hornets ...

5

Make the most of every opportunity in these evil days.

Ephesians 5:16 NLT

"Are You in the Clutter Club?"

*I*s your life cluttered? Do you have too much stuff going on in your life? Do you leave the house early in the morning and arrive back home just in time to go to bed? If so, you are definitely a member of The Clutter Club. And, you're not alone. Probably many of your friends are members of that same club. With practices, games, more practices, more games, homework, school, more homework, church, Drama club, student council meetings (oh, and let's not forget the hours spent texting, editing your Instagram pics, and updating your

Facebook status), there's not much time for anything else.

You know what happens when you have too much clutter in your life? You get stressed out, and then you freak out! One day your best friend says, "Hey, how come you didn't text back last night?" and you bite her head off with, "Hello! I have like a million things to do. You're not the center of my world!"

Yikes!

Not good. You need to de-clutter your life.

I've got good news for you. God is the King of de-cluttering. He is the best organizer, the best planner, the best at time management (I mean, hey, He created the whole world in less than a week!), the best at everything. He will help you get rid of, organize, and prioritize your life—just ask Him.

The Bible says to seek Him first. When you do that, all of the clutter just seems to fall off, and God supernaturally organizes your day. So, talk to Him right now. Ask the Father to de-clutter your life, and get ready to join a different club—"The Clutter-free Chicks." Whoo hoo! ☺

STRENGTH TRAINING: *Don't be like the people of this world, but let God change the way you think. Then you will know how to do everything that is good and pleasing to him* (Romans 12:2 CEV).

MEGAPHONE TO MASTER: "Lord, thank You for de-cluttering my life. Amen."

FIRE UP!: Do you have way too much going on in your life? How much "downtime/free time" do you have? Is there anything you can cut out from your life to make it less cluttered?

GIVE A SHOUT!: "I will de-clutter my life."

READY. OK: Grab your journal and write down some of the things in your life that are cluttering it up. Now, mark through the ones that you wouldn't mind getting rid of.

JUMP INTO ACTION!: Look for ways to de-clutter your life this week. Maybe you can drop one or two activities from your schedule? Ask your parents and the Lord to help you make those decisions.

FAST FACT:

Did you know that on Nov. 6, 1869, the first intercollegiate football game took place between Princeton and Rutgers and the original "Sis Boom Bah!" cheer was shouted by the fans?

FIT TIP:

More core work? Of course! Lie on the mat face up, place your hands behind your head (don't lace your fingers), and support your neck. Push the small of your back into the mat and suck in your abs. Lift your knees into your chest while lifting your shoulder blades off the floor. Rotate to the right, bringing the left elbow towards the right knee while extending the other leg into the air. Then, reverse the move and continue alternating these bicycle movements for 12 to 15 reps on each side.

Here's another fun chant to try with your squad …

Here We Go!

Here we go, Big Blue! (x)
Keep it up, Eagles.
Shoot for two! (xx)
(Repeat)

*(x) = pause.

*Insert your school's mascot for "Eagles" in this chant and your school's main color for "blue."

6

I run toward the goal, so that I can win the prize of being called to heaven. This is the prize that God offers because of what Christ Jesus has done.

Philippians 3:14 CEV

"A Little Competition ..."

Competition is good. It makes us better athletes. It makes us try harder. It makes us push ourselves past the point that we thought physically possible. Yes, competition is a good thing. Unless ... you allow it to eat you up inside. Once that happens, competition becomes a bad thing. Ever happened to you?

It often happens to top athletes. You've been trained to win. Winning is the ultimate goal, so your competitor becomes your ultimate enemy. You'll do whatever it takes to beat that person or that team. The competition itself is no longer fun. Even when you win, you can't enjoy the moment. Nope. You're too worried about the next competitor and getting another victory. No time to celebrate. You have to move on and prepare for the next competition. Scary, isn't it?

If you're on this "competition merry-go-round," it's time to jump off. After all, sports competition is supposed to be fun. You need to take time to do that victory dance. You need to celebrate your victories and learn from your losses. But, if you're so consumed with winning that next cheer trophy or claiming a spot at Cheer Nationals that you can't enjoy the journey on the way to victory, then you need some God time. Ask Him to help you enjoy the process—not just the outcome. Let competition drive you, but don't let it consume you. Remember, winning isn't everything. Besides, God already says you're a winner.

STRENGTH TRAINING: *You know that many runners enter a race, and only one of them wins the prize* (1 Corinthians 9:24, CEV).

FIRE UP!: So, are you totally obsessed with winning? Are you consumed with your next cheer competition? If you lose, are you going to be totally upset? If you answered "yes" to any of those questions, ask God to change your heart so that winning isn't the most important thing in your life.

MEGAPHONE TO MASTER: "God, help me to enjoy the journey—not just the victories. Amen."

GIVE A SHOUT!: Say out loud: "I am a winner in God's eyes."

READY. OK: Grab your journal and write down your biggest accomplishment. Now, write down your greatest fear. Are they related? Does your fear have anything to do with losing? Take time to praise God for your accomplishments and give Him all of your fears.

JUMP INTO ACTION: Think back ... have you acted ugly in the past when you've lost? Did you take time to congratulate the winning cheer team? The next time you have the chance to say, "Good job!" to one of your competitors, just do it! Be a good winner and a good loser.

FAST FACT:

Did you know that when cheerleading first began, cheerleaders were called yell leaders?

FIT TIP:

If your squad is using the weight room these days or you're embarking on a strength training program all on your own, make sure you warm up with five to ten minutes of cardio before each strength training session and make sure you stretch after!

Here's a new cheer to try with your squad …

Get On Up!

Get on up! Are you ready? (clap, clap)
Are you ready (x) to fight?
Let's hear it for the Wildcats.
Let's win (x) tonight.

Get on up! Are you ready? (clap, clap)
Are you ready (x) to fight?
Let's hear it for the Wildcats!
Yell purple, gold, and white.
Purple, gold, and white.
Purple, gold, and white!

*(x) = pause

*Put your school's colors in place of purple, gold, and white and your school's mascot in place of Wildcats …

7

*And whatever you do, in word or deed, do everything
in the name of the Lord Jesus, giving thanks to God the
Father through him.*

Colossians 3:17 ESV

"Giving It Your All!"

*D*o you give it your all every time you go to cheer
practice, and every time you take the floor for cheer
competition, and every time you cheer on your team
from the sidelines? Or, do you only work hard when
the coach is looking over your shoulder or you're per-
forming in front of all of your peers?

If you only work hard and give it your all when all
eyes are on you, then you may have an integrity problem. Dictionary.com defines integrity as: "Steadfast ad-
herence to a strict moral or ethical code." OK, so that's a

lot of big words that actually mean: you do what you're supposed to do—the best you can—no matter what.

Just think if every girl on your team only did her best when the spotlight was shining on her. Your team would never have an all-out practice because the spotlight can't be on every girl, all the time. There are going to be times when you aren't in the front row of the routine. There are going to be times when you aren't given a special part. But that's OK. Do whatever your part is—full out—to the best of your ability every time. See, if you're not giving it your all each time you work out with your cheer team, your lack of effort can potentially mess up the whole practice. And, that's not fair.

Here's a little secret. Even when you think your coach isn't watching, your coach probably is. I am a coach, and let me tell you this—I'm always watching. I observe who gives it everything she's got during practice. Why? Well, she is the one I'm going to call on when game day rolls around because I know I can depend on her to do her best—no matter what. That's the kind of unselfish, all-out athlete that coaches love. So, give it your all every single time. Don't wait until you're in the spotlight before you show your best effort. Walk in integrity. Do your best even if no one is watching because Someone is always watching. God will honor your integrity. He knows what it's like to give your best. He's been doing that for us since the beginning of time.

STRENGTH TRAINING: *But as for you, brethren, do not grow weary in doing good* (2 Thessalonians 3:13 NKJV).

FIRE UP!: Be honest, do you do your very best even when no one is watching? If not, ask yourself why?

MEGAPHONE TO MASTER: "God, help me to do my best—no matter what. Amen."

GIVE A SHOUT!: Say out loud: "I will give it my all every single day, in every single way."

READY. OK: Take a moment and write down a time when you remember giving it your all—maybe it was at a game or practice. Now, write down how that made you feel. Were you proud? Satisfied? Angry because no one noticed? Now, write this next to your observations: "I do everything for God." That's what you have to remember each time you practice or compete.

JUMP INTO ACTION: Decide today to practice and compete the best you can—no matter who is watching. If you need a reminder, make a little sign to keep in your locker that says, "Do it unto God." You'll know what it means! ☺

FAST FACT:

Did you know that according to "The Complete Guide to Cheerleading", organized cheering started at Princeton University in 1884?

FIT TIP:

Lie face down on your stability ball, with the ball just below your knees. Put your hands on the floor in a push-up position. Now, slowly lower yourself toward the floor and then back up to your starting position. Do 10 to 15 reps. Your arms and chest will thank you!

Here's another chant to try with your squad …

Rock With The Red!

Gotta rock with the red
And roll with the white!
Yell: Go, Cougars! Fight! (x)
(crowd repeats: "Go Cougars, fight!")
(x)

*Insert your school's mascot for "Cougars" and your school's colors for "red and white" in this chant.

*(x) = pause.

8

Christ gives me the strength to face anything.

Philippians 4:13 CEV

"Don't Worry, Be Happy!"

The biggest cheer competition of the year is coming up. You've only landed your round-off back-handspring back tuck a few times, yet your coach has put it in the routine. She says you can do it. You're not too sure. So, what do you do? If you're like many athletes, you worry. But, worry never produces good results. All worry does is invite its good friends, fear and doubt, into your mind, and they stay in there and party—making you totally miserable and unsure of your abilities.

The Bible says, *God is striding ahead of you. He's right there with you. He won't let you down; he won't leave you. Don't be intimidated. Don't worry* (Deuteronomy 31:8 MSG).

Worry only fuels fear and doubt—fear of failure and doubt in your abilities. Instead of letting worry rule your mind, kick it out! Don't meditate on the "what ifs" of life. Instead, think about winning. See yourself doing your very best job. See yourself landing that back tuck. This is called visualization, and it's a biblical principle. Ask God to help you overcome your worries and fears, and ask Him to replace them with His supernatural confidence and strength. He will! So, don't worry—be happy!

STRENGTH TRAINING: *Give your entire attention to what God is doing right now, and don't get worked up about what may or may not happen tomorrow. God will help you deal with whatever hard things come up when the time comes* (Matthew 6:34 MSG).

FIRE UP!: Do you worry a lot before a big competition? If so, why?

MEGAPHONE TO MASTER: "God, I give all of my worries to You. Please give me Your strength and Your supernatural confidence. Amen."

GIVE A SHOUT!: Say out loud: "I will not worry, and I will not be afraid. I can do all things through Christ who gives me strength."

READY. OK: Grab your journal and write down your greatest worries—no matter what they are. Maybe you're worried about an upcoming competition. Maybe you're worried you won't make good enough grades this grading term. Maybe you're worried that your parents will get divorced. List your worries and then write over the top of them in red ink: God is more than enough! I will not fear! Let this be a reminder that you don't have to worry. God has your back!

JUMP INTO ACTION: The next time you feel worry on the inside of you—stop, drop and pray. Don't dwell on the worry. Meditate on God and His strength and ability. Ask Him to take away your worries and fill you with God confidence.

FAST FACT:

Did you know that the "Olympics" of All-star cheerleading is called Worlds?

FIT TIP:

Listen to me—thin doesn't always equal healthy! Unfortunately, Anorexia Nervosa is common in sports such as cheerleading, dance, gymnastics, figure skating, track, and wrestling. If you are struggling with this, or if someone on your squad is eerily thin and rarely eats or becomes super obsessed with body image, reach out to your coach or a counselor at school or your parents or a pastor.

Don't let Anorexia steal one more day of joy and health from your life. God has a better way, and He has a way of escape for you or your friend who is battling this disorder. For more information, go to nationaleatingdisorders.org or call 800-931-2237 for a list of professionals in your area.

Here's an offense chant to try with your squad (for football, say "6" for basketball say "2") …

Let's Up That Score!

Six more! (x)
Six more! (xx)
C'mon Hornets, let's up that score!
(repeat)

*(x) = pause.

*Insert your school's mascot for "Hornets."

9

Don't be jealous or proud, but be humble and consider others more important than yourselves.

Philippians 2:3 CEV

"Don't Be Jealous!"

Face it—she's better than you. She jumps higher. She tumbles better. Her motions are sharper. She's just a better cheerleader. It's tough, isn't it? No matter how hard you work, she's just better. She has a natural ability that shines. It seems like no matter what she tries, it comes easily to her. And, to top it all off, the guy you sort of like doesn't like you. He likes her! Ugh!

That's usually when the green-eyed monster shows up.

Jealousy. Yep, it's a hard emotion to control. As athletes, we're competitive people. It's just who we are, so when someone is better than us, we can become too competitive. That "too competitive spirit" can easily turn into jealousy.

Ever been there?

No matter what sport you play or where you play it, there will always be someone better than you. That's just life. In addition, there will also always be someone prettier, smarter, richer, taller, thinner, etc. Don't let that drive you crazy with jealousy. Just accept that fact and forget about those who are "better." Set your sights on becoming the best version of you. You don't need to worry about anyone else. Concentrate on doing your best every time you compete. Don't focus on your flaws. Focus on your positive traits. You are unique! God made you special. You have wonderful talents and strengths. So, the next time that green-eyed monster rears his ugly head, turn your head upward and thank God for making you—you!

STRENGTH TRAINING: *Love is kind and patient, never jealous, boastful, proud, or rude* (1 Corinthians 13:4-5 CEV).

FIRE UP!: Is there someone you are jealous of right now? If so, ask yourself—why?

MEGAPHONE TO MASTER: "Father God, I admit that I am jealous sometimes. Please help me stop feeling jealous and just focus on being the best version of me."

GIVE A SHOUT!: Say out loud: "I will stop comparing myself to others. I will celebrate the person You made me to be."

READY. OK: It's journal time. Describe a time when you felt very jealous of someone. Now write the advice you would give to a friend who was going through the same situation. What would you tell her? How would you tell her to fight off the jealous feelings she was having?

JUMP INTO ACTION: The best way to get rid of jealousy? Stop comparing yourself to others. Why? Because there will always be someone you won't measure up to in your mind. If there is one certain person who really brings out that "green-eyed monster" in you, be extra kind to her. The next time she does well or wins an award, send her a little "congrats" card.

FAST FACT:

Did you know that the board game Monopoly has an All-star cheerleading version?

FIT TIP:

To make your toe touches better, sit on the floor in a straddle position while watching your shows that you

DVR'd earlier. The more you stretch, the better your jumps will be!

Here's an offense chant to try with your squad:

Touchdown, Let's Score!

Down the field, we want six!
Touchdown!
(x)
Let's score!
(x)
(repeat)

*You can use this for football or basketball. For football, do it just like it's written here. For basketball, say "Down the floor, we want two! Basket! Let's score!"

*(x) = pause.

10

Am I now trying to win the approval of human beings, or of God? Or am I trying to please people?

Galatians 1:10, NIV

"Are You A Perfectionist?"

"**Hey!** You did so great on your cross tumbling pass tonight!" shouts your friend after your cheer squad's halftime performance. "You were awesome!"

"Thanks," you mumble, "but I totally opened up too soon on my tuck. I landed it weird."

Does this conversation sound familiar?

Do you know the problem with always trying to be perfect? You always end up disappointed in yourself and others. No matter how hard you practice. No matter how hard you train. No matter how much you want it. You'll never be perfect.

If you're a perfectionist—especially when it comes to athletics—you probably feel like you're not good enough. It's tough to accept a less-than-perfect performance, but once you understand that perfection is only a goal—not a requirement—you'll be a lot happier in all that you do.

So, go ahead and shoot for perfection, but don't beat yourself up when you don't meet those impossible goals. Instead, celebrate the goals you do reach. Maybe you haven't nailed your standing back tuck yet, but your backhand spring series are way faster than they used to be. Don't dwell on the fact that you can't throw a standing back tuck yet. Instead, celebrate your improvement on your standing series.

See, God wants you to celebrate the "you" that He made you to be. He doesn't expect you to be perfect all the time, so why should you expect perfection from yourself? God knows you are human. After all, He made you! Ask Him to help you feel happier with yourself. And, start celebrating the winner God made you to be. You may never be perfect, but you are perfectly loved by God.

STRENGTH TRAINING: *Nothing is completely perfect, except your teachings* (Psalm 119:96 CEV).

Nothing on earth is totally perfect, except for God's Word. He is perfect, and His Word is perfect, and He loves you—no matter your imperfections. Now that's something to cheer about!

FIRE UP!: Do you expect perfection of yourself? When you fall short of the goals you set, do you feel really bad about yourself?

MEGAPHONE TO MASTER: "God, I am constantly upset with myself because I'm not perfect in every area. Help me to be satisfied with the person you made me to be. Thanks for loving me. Amen."

GIVE A SHOUT!: Say out loud: "I may not be perfect, but I am perfectly loved by God."

READY. OK: Grab your journal and write two goals you'd like to achieve this week. You can write anything. For example, maybe you want to shoot for 75 sit-ups each day, as you strengthen your core. Or, maybe you'd like to hit that lib you've been working on forever. Whatever your goals are, they are important to God because you are important to God. Be sure to check off your goals when you reach them .... and set new ones each week!

JUMP INTO ACTION: If you're feeling less than perfect today—guess what? You're not alone. Lots of people feel that way. Look around you today and see if you can identify someone who is being too hard on herself. Maybe your best friend? Maybe your coach? Find an opportunity to congratulate that person on something today. Let her know that you think she's awesome, and remind her that God thinks so, too!

FAST FACT:

Did you know that Actress Dakota Fanning was once a high school cheerleader?

FIT TIP:

Squats are great for strengthening and toning your lower body. So, start with your feet shoulder-width apart, chest up, shoulders back, and arms straight out to your side at shoulder height. Keep your heels on the floor, bend your knees and squat down, sinking your weight into your heels. Next, lift up your body (pushing from your heels) and return to standing position. Do one set of 15 reps.

Here's a new cheer to try with your squad …

We Want It More!

Hey (x) we're back.
And better than before.
Purple and gold
(x)

Are taking back the floor.
Tigers (x) that's right,
We want it more!

*(x) = pause

* Put your school's colors in place of purple and gold
and your school's mascot in place of Tigers.

11

*Finally, brethren, whatever things are true, whatever
things are noble, whatever things are just, whatever
things are pure, whatever things are lovely, whatever
things are of good report, if there is any virtue and if there
is anything praiseworthy—meditate on these things.*

Philippians 4:8 NKJV

"Watch Your Words!"

*I*t's the final game of your school's boys' basketball
tourney, and your coach has decided your cheer team
will perform your competition routine during halftime.
You haven't performed that routine in a few months, so
you're super nervous. The music starts, and you're off.
You bust onto the scene with your first tumbling pass,
and you totally nail it. The crowd is cheering, and you're
feeling good about the performance.

You push yourself even harder as you power through the high-energy routine, remembering to smile and perform as if it were Cheer Worlds. Then, it's over. You look up to see everyone clapping. It's an awesome moment. Your family and friends all congratulate you, telling you how great you performed. Your teammates give you high fives for nailing the difficult tumbling pass. Then, your coach says, "Your tuck wasn't very tight on your tumbling pass. Your landing would've been better if your tuck had been tighter."

Ugh.

The coach's words hurt. Suddenly, you've forgotten all of the nice things that were said to you. Instead, your mind thinks about the coach's stinging words. Your great performance is overshadowed by one negative comment.

Ever happened to you?

If so, you're not alone. We tend to focus on the negative comments people make to us more than the positive ones. While it may be difficult to do, you need to shake off the negative comments and think of the good ones. If there is some sort of constructive criticism within that negative comment, then take that part of it, make the necessary adjustments, and simply move forward.

Words are quite powerful. They have the power to tear down or build up. In other words, you can either make somebody's day with your words or destroy somebody's day with your words. It's your choice.

Start using your words wisely, building up those around you. Look for opportunities to encourage your fellow athletes, friends, family, teachers, coaches, etc. Just think—your positive comment may be the only one that person has heard all week. So, make a difference with your mouth today!

STRENGTH TRAINING: *For out of the overflow of his heart his mouth speaks* (Luke 6:45, NIV).

FIRE UP!: Have your words been the building-up kind or the tearing-down kind today?

MEGAPHONE TO MASTER: "God, put a watch over my mouth so that I only speak good things to those around me. Help me to be a builder with my words, not one who tears down. And, help me not focus on the negative things others say about me, but help me focus on what Your Word says about me. I love You. Amen."

GIVE A SHOUT!: Say out loud: "I will use my words to build people up, not tear them down."

READY. OK: Grab your journal and your Bible and write down three things God says about you in His Word. Here is one to get you started: You are the apple of His eye! Not sure how to find these truths? You can simply go to Google search and type in, "What does the Bible say about me being special?" and lots of websites will pop up with scriptures for you. ☺

JUMP INTO ACTION: Look for chances to build up others with your words this week. Ask God to help you.

FAST FACT:

Did you know that the first cheer squads were made up of all males?

FIT TIP:

When training, make sure you vary your workouts. If you always do the exact same routine, your body will get used to it, and you'll stop seeing results. So, switch it up! Variety is more fun anyway!

Here's a new cheer to try with your squad …

Better Than The Rest!

Determined and driven.
The Cats are the best!
We're number one, that's right!
(x)
Better than the rest!

(x)
Get ready to cheer
For the red, white, and blue!
The best, you know it!
And, we're coming after you!

*(x) = pause

*Put your school's colors in place of red, white, and blue
and your school's mascot in place of Cats.

12

In fact, God thinks of us as a perfume that brings Christ to everyone.

2 Corinthians 2:15 NIV

"Do You Smell Like Dirty Cheer Socks?"

*Y*ou unzip your cheer bag to grab your pom-pons, and suddenly, an odor attacks you. It's the worst smell ever. It reeks like something has died inside your bag. With further investigation, you discover the source of the stinky-ness—your dirty, sweaty old cheer socks. That's when you finally remember—you were supposed to take those dirty socks home weeks ago for Mom to wash them. But, you kept forgetting, and now they're stinking up the place!

That's what happens when you don't wash stuff. It gets super dirty and stinks worse than Aunt Bessie's breath. Well, guess what? If you don't wash your heart in the Word of God on a regular basis, you'll start to stink, too.

According to 2 Corinthians 2:15, we're supposed to give off the aroma of Christ to all who meet us. In other words, if you haven't spent time reading the Bible and letting God's Word wash over your heart, you won't give off a good aroma to those around you. We have to spend time reading the Bible and praying so that God can clean us up on the inside and leave us "smelling" just like Him.

When you spend time with God, you'll become like God. You'll even "smell" like God. But, if you don't spend time with Him, you'll begin to stink even worse than your old cheer socks.

So, don't go around stinking up the world. (Trust me, there's not enough Bath & Body Works potions to cover up that stench!) Instead, spend time reading God's Word and praying to Him. Let God turn your stinky heart into a pure, clean, and sweet-smelling heart. (Oh, and don't forget to take home those cheer socks and wash them!)

STRENGTH TRAINING: *With my whole heart I have sought You; Oh, let me not wander from Your com-*

mandments! Your word I have hidden in my heart, That I might not sin against You (Psalm 119:10-11 NKJV).

FIRE UP!: So, be honest. Does your heart need a good cleaning? Does it smell like your dirty cheer socks?

MEGAPHONE TO MASTER: "God, I want to become more like You in every way. Clean up my heart, Lord, and help me to become a sweet fragrance of You. Amen."

GIVE A SHOUT!: Say out loud: "I am the aroma of Christ!"

READY. OK: It's journal time. Write a contract with God, promising to spend at least 10 minutes a day reading the Bible. Then sign it and date it. Now it's official!

JUMP INTO ACTION: Find 10 minutes in your busy schedule for God. Maybe you could get up 10 minutes earlier for school? Or maybe you could read your Bible 10 minutes right before you go to bed? Get a game plan and get reading!

FAST FACT:

Did you know that in a correct toe touch jump, you don't really touch your toes?

FIT TIP:

When stretching, make sure you never bounce.
Instead, do a static stretch, slowly leaning into
the stretch and holding it.

Here's a new defense chant to try with your squad
during football season …

Push 'Em Back!

Push 'em back!
Hold 'em back!
Go Panthers Go!
(x)
(repeat)

*(x) = pause or clap.

*Put your school's mascot in place of "Panthers."

13

...And let us run with endurance the race
God has set before us.

Hebrews 12:1 NLT

"Just Warming Up ..."

Have you ever arrived late to a game and missed the warm-up stretches and drills? Your fellow cheerleaders are all throwing their standing back handsprings, and you're just trying to get your uniform on. You're so late there's not time to do all the stretches and exercises you normally do, so you rush through a few stretching moves and join your squad on the floor. Then, only a few minutes into the game, your muscles start cramping, and you feel like you're going to die. That's because you didn't take enough time to properly stretch and warm up your muscles.

It's the exact same way in our lives as Christians. Did you know that? We have to take time to "warm up" with God so that we'll be ready for the game of life. Warming up involves reading the Bible every day, praying to God often, and going to church regularly. If we do those things consistently, we'll be spiritually fit and ready to do what God needs us to do whenever He needs us to do it.

Think of God as your Coach. He may want to call on you to witness to your friend or help someone who needs some encouragement, but if you're not spiritually warmed up, He will have to pass you over and call on someone who is already warmed up. Don't be left warming the bench. Instead, get spiritually warmed up and ready for God to use you!

STRENGTH TRAINING: *Preach the word! Be ready in season and out of season* (2 Timothy 4:2 NKJV).

FIRE UP!: Think about yourself … are you spiritually warmed up right now? Or, are you a "pulled spiritual muscle" just waiting to happen?

MEGAPHONE TO MASTER: "God, I want to be your go-to girl. I want to be ready to be used— whenever you need me. Help me to get spiritually fit so that You can call on me anytime You want. I love You. Amen."

GIVE A SHOUT!: Say out loud: "I am warmed up and ready to be used by my Heavenly Father."

READY. OK: It's journal time. Write a plan for becoming spiritually warmed up. Find time in your schedule to read God's Word, pray, and go to church. Ask God to help you find that time and stick to your plan.

JUMP INTO ACTION: Get a spiritual fitness buddy and start the buddy check system. You two could read the Bible together, pray together, and even go to church together. Or, at least you could keep track of each other's spiritual progress. Check up on each other! Before long, you'll both be spiritually warmed up and ready to go!

FAST FACT:

Did you know that the correct term is not "pompoms"; it's pompons?

FIT TIP:

When working on your jumps, keep your chest up and your toes pointed.

Here's a new chant to try with your squad …

Spirit!

S-S-S P-I!
R-R-R I-T!
S-P-I
R-I-T
Spirit, we've got spirit!
(repeat)

14

*"For I know the plans I have for you," says the L*ORD*.*
"They are plans for good and not for disaster, to give you a
future and a hope."

Jeremiah 29:11 NLT

"Whatever!"

*Y*our coach tells you to spit out your gum or leave practice, and you mumble under your breath, "Whatever." Your best friend says, "I don't like your new cheer bow. It's not as cute as the sparkly silver one you wore last week to practice," and you make the little "W" sign with your hands and say, "Whatever."

Saying, "whatever" is probably not the best way to show a good attitude. But, if you're like most of your peers, you probably say it several times a day. It seems to be quite popular these days. Who would have thought that the ever-popular "whatever" could actually help you memorize a wonderful scripture? Philippians 4:8 tells us that we should think about WHATEVER is true, noble, right, pure, lovely, admirable, excellent, and praiseworthy. That's a mouthful, eh?

It's a mind full, too. If you fill your mind with all of those good things, you won't be able to think about bad stuff, like the back tuck you over-rotated at last night's game, falling right on your bum, the fight you had with your best friend, or the fact that you weren't chosen for the "A" All-star cheer team. You need to think about your strengths. God wants you to see yourself the same way that He sees you. And, He thinks you're amazing!

If you constantly think about your weaknesses, you'll never achieve all that God has for you. That's why you should do what Philippians 4:8 says, and think about good stuff. Don't waste your time on the negative stuff. You've got too many good things to think about. Jeremiah 29:11 tells us that God has a good plan for your life. So, think about that—the Creator of the Universe has big plans for you! That's a reason for another "W" word—WOW!

STRENGTH TRAINING: *Finally, brothers, whatever is true, whatever is noble, whatever is right, whatever is pure, whatever is lovely, whatever is admirable—if anything is excellent or praiseworthy—think about such things* (Philippians 4:8 NIV).

FIRE UP!: Do you tend to think about bad stuff? What can you do to stop thinking about negative things and start thinking about good things?

MEGAPHONE TO MASTER: "Father, I have a bad habit of thinking about bad stuff, but I don't want to do that anymore. Lord, help me to only think of good things. I want to be a positive person. Help me to achieve all that You have for me. I love You, Amen."

GIVE A SHOUT!: "I will think on good things; I will be a positive person."

READY. OK: OK girls, get out your journals and write one good thing that begins with each letter—something positive in your life that you can think about. For instance, for your "W" letter, you might write "Winner" because that's how God sees you. Get the idea?

W

H

A

T

E

V

E

R

JUMP INTO ACTION: While saying "whatever" can be fun, just make sure you're not saying it too often and in a disrespectful way. Ask a close friend to help you keep track of how often you say "whatever" in a day. You might be surprised …

FAST FACT:

Did you know that a 360 down is another name for a twist cradle?

FIT TIP:

To work your calves, stand on the edge of a step and raise onto your toes and then lower back down. Do 25 reps if you can, and don't rush them.

Here's a new chant to try with your squad.

BASKET CATS BASKET!

B-A-S
K-E-T
Basket, Cats, basket!
(x)

(repeat)

*(x) = pause or clap.

*Put your school's mascot in place of "Cats."

15

Faith is the confidence that what we hope for will actually happen; it gives us assurance about things we cannot see.

Hebrews 11:1 NLT

"Blind Faith"

*Y*our school's girls' basketball team is not playing well. In fact, your team hasn't scored in what seems like years, leaving your squad very little to cheer about. Still, you keep cheering, supporting your team, and hoping for a miracle. Just then, your girls' basketball coach does something you don't understand or agree with—he benches the best player on your team.

"What is he thinking?" you whisper to one of your fellow cheerleaders. "Is he crazy? We DEFINITELY can't win without her in the game!"

Just like you thought, your team loses—big time.

You're sure your team might have had a chance for a comeback if only coach would've played your star athlete. But, she finished the game on the bench. You don't understand. You're mad at the coach.

You think about the coach's decision for days, wondering why he would do something so stupid. The whole school is talking about it. Then, you find out. Your coach benched your star player to protect her from injury. The other team was playing really rough, and several members of your team had already been hurt during the game. He didn't want to risk another injury—especially your star player—with the tournament coming up. You discover it was actually a good decision—even though it didn't seem like one at the time.

Guess what? It's the same way with God. He does things that we don't always understand. The Bible says that God's ways are higher than ours. In other words, we may not always understand why God does what He does, but we can be sure of one thing—He is always looking out for us because He wants what is best for us.

So, even when it looks like He isn't working things out for you, trust Him anyway. Walk in blind faith. He has you covered!

STRENGTH TRAINING: *Jesus said to him, "Have you believed because you have seen me? Blessed are those who have not seen and you have believed* (John 20:29 ESV).

FIRE UP!: Do you trust God—even when you don't understand what is going on around you?

MEGAPHONE TO MASTER: "God, help me to trust You in all situations. Help me to be reminded that Your ways are higher than my ways. Amen."

GIVE A SHOUT!: "I will trust God even when I don't understand."

READY. OK: OK girls, get your journals and write something going on in your life right now that you simply don't understand. Now, write on top of it with a red marker, "But I choose to trust You anyway, God."

JUMP INTO ACTION: The next time your coach or your parents or someone else in your life makes a decision you don't understand, why not pray for that person? Learn to believe the best in others. Ask God to help you.

FAST FACT:

Did you know that the most important tip you can give a flyer on your team is simply: stay tight?

FIT TIP:

Push-ups are great for strengthening your arms and chest area, but not everyone can do the traditional "boy" ones. If doing them on your toes are too difficult, do "girl" push-ups by dropping to your knees and doing push-ups from that position. Also, if you don't have a mat, you can do push-ups on the wall. To increase difficulty, move your feet farther away from the wall.

Here's a new chant to try with your squad.

RED, WHITE GO COUGARS!

Red, white, go Cougars!
(x)
Go, Go Cougars!
(x)
(repeat)

*(x) = pause or clap.

*Put your school's mascot in place of "Cougars" and your school's colors in place of "red and white."

16

Bless those who persecute you. Don't curse them;
pray that God will bless them.

Romans 12:14 NLT

"Say What?"

"*Y*our scorpion is embarrassing!" yells Macy, the other flyer on your cheer team. "Want me to show you how it's done?"

You try to ignore her, but she keeps talking trash to you.

You're so mad you could just, just, just ... pray for her!

Say what?

I know. I know. It seems totally weird to pray for someone who has hurt your feelings. It seems dumb to pray for that person who enjoys being mean to you. It just seems wrong to pray for that coach who embarrasses you every day in practice. But, it's what Jesus said to do in His Word. He said to pray for your enemies. He didn't say you had to like it, but He did say you had to do it.

On your own, you probably can't pray for your enemies, but you don't have to depend on your own strength. God will help you. So, the next time one of your teammates acts ugly to you during practice, don't fight back. Instead, pray for her. You probably won't feel like praying for her at that very moment, but do it anyway. Pray for your enemies by faith. You may have to do it through gritted teeth and with a red face but pray anyway. If you'll do your part, God will do His. He may not change your enemy's actions, but He will change the way you feel about that enemy. So, determine today to pray—especially for your enemies!

STRENGTH TRAINING: *But I tell you who hear me: Love your enemies, do good to those who hate you, bless those who curse you, pray for those who mistreat you* (Luke 6:27-28, NIV).

FIRE UP!: Do you have enemies? Do you ever pray for them?

MEGAPHONE TO MASTER: "Lord, change my heart. Help me not to fight back against my enemies. Help me to pray for them instead. I love You, Lord. Amen."

GIVE A SHOUT!: "I will pray for my enemies. I will kill them with kindness."

READY. OK: Let's face it. "Love your enemies" is one of the toughest commandments that Jesus gave to us. It goes against everything we feel, but it's the only way to change your heart toward the enemies in your life. So, right now, grab that journal and write down the first names of the enemies in your life. This is now your prayer list!

JUMP INTO ACTION: Now, say this prayer, putting all of their names in each of the blanks.

"Lord, I thank You for Your love. Help me to love _____ today. Help me to see _____ through Your eyes. And, Lord, please help me not to be hurt by _____'s words and actions. Guard my heart, Lord, and change it, too. I pray that You bless _____ today and help _____ with whatever is troubling her/him. Thank You for loving me and loving _____, too. In Jesus' Mighty Name. Amen."

Now, keep saying this prayer. Say it daily. Say it every time you think about that person or those people. Keep on praying that God will change the situation in your favor.

FAST FACT:

Did you know that "Go, Fight, Win"
is the most common chant?

FIT TIP:

Want more defined arms? How about trying some tricep
dips? You'll need a step or a platform of some kind that's
about a foot or two off of the ground. (Folded mats would
work!) Place your hands on the step or mats with your
body straight out in front of you. (Your back should be
facing the platform or stacked mats.) Next, bend your
arms until your booty is almost touching the ground, and
then push back up! Try doing eight to 10 reps.

Here's another chant to try with your squad …

One We Are The Cougars!

One, we are the Cougars!
Two, a little bit louder!
Three, we still can't hear you
Four, more, more, more!
(repeat)

*Put your school's mascot in place of "Cougars."

17

Work willingly at whatever you do, as though you were

working for the Lord rather than for people.

Colossians 3:23 NLT

"Be On Time"

*P*unctuality. Just reading the word might be painful for you—especially if you're one of those people who is always late. Are your friends constantly waiting on you? Do you show up late for practice on a regular basis? Being on time is a tough one, but it's also very necessary. If you're always late, it will get you into trouble, and it will really hurt your Christian witness.

Someone once said, "By being late, you are disrespecting everyone who has to wait for you."

Ouch. That one really hits home, doesn't it? Punctuality counts. If you're always late, ask God to help you. And, then try these things to get you out the door on time.

*Set your clock 15 minutes ahead of time.

*Get all of your stuff together the night before and place it by the door.

*Lay out your clothes the night before—down to your socks, shoes, and cheer bow. (This goes for your practice clothes, too!)

*Get a friend to be your punctuality partner— someone to help you keep your promise to be on time.

*Don't try to do too much before you head out the door.

*Pray that God will help you with your tardiness.

God wants to be involved in every part of your life. Being on time may seem like a small matter, but God wants you to be excellent in all areas of your life. Don't let tardiness hurt your witness. Making these small changes can make a big difference in your life and the lives of those around you. So, go ahead and talk to God about helping you in the area of punctuality. He's got the time.

STRENGTH TRAINING: *There is a time for everything, and a season for every activity under heaven* (Ecclesiastes 3:1 NIV).

FIRE UP!: When is the last time you were late to be somewhere? What caused you to be late? Was it just a one-time thing or are you perpetually late?

MEGAPHONE TO MASTER: "Lord, help me to be more punctual. Help me to make it a habit of being on time. Thanks for caring about even the small concerns in my life. In the Mighty Name of Jesus, Amen."

GIVE A SHOUT!: "I will be on time today. I can do this."

READY. OK: If you don't have a daily planner, maybe you should consider getting one. Or if you have a smartphone, you probably have a calendar and a way to keep track of your appointments on there. Use your journal time today to plug in your upcoming practices, games, competitions, class assignments, etc. Seeing them on a calendar will help you budget your time and plan to be punctual. ☺

JUMP INTO ACTION: If you do something 14 days in a row, it will become a habit. At least, that's what the experts say. So, try your very best to be on time for everything for two whole weeks.

FAST FACT:

Did you know that in Norway, toe touches are often called tiptoes?

FIT TIP:

Drink up! Did you know that many times we eat because we think we are hungry when we are actually dehydrated? Some nutritionists say that we need 64 ounces of water each day. So, make sure you keep your water bottle full and keep refilling it! You need water to stay healthy and energized!

Here's another chant to try with your squad …

Celebrate!

Celebrate, the Cats are great!
Yell, "Go Big Blue!"
(x)
(crowd repeats, "Go Big Blue!")
(x)
(repeat)

*(x) = pause or clap. Put your school's mascot in place of "Cats" and your school's main color in place of "blue."

18

They gave Moses this account: "We went into the land to which you sent us, and it does flow with milk and honey! Here is its fruit. But the people who live there are powerful, and the cities are fortified and very large. We even saw descendants of Anak there."

Numbers 13:27-28 NIV

"Watch Those 'Buts'"

One of my favorite Bible teachers once said, "Everything after the 'but' in a statement pretty much cancels out what came before it ..." After hearing that, I started taking notice of all the "buts" in life—even the "buts" I come across when reading the Bible. One particular "but" really stood out to me as I read the story of the 12 spies.

Remember that one?

God told Moses to send out 12 men—one from each tribe—to scout out the land of Canaan and its people. So, the 12 spies journeyed to Canaan and spent 40 days studying the area and the people who occupied it before returning to Moses. The 12 spies brought back a sample of the land's fruit (the grapes were so large that it took two men to carry just one cluster!) as well as a thorough report of what they had seen.

Ten of the spies said: *Look at this fruit! The land we explored is rich with milk and honey. But the people who live there are strong, and their cities are large and walled* ... (Numbers 13:27-28, CEV).

Notice the "but."

In other words, "Yeah, we found the land to be flowing with milk and honey, exactly as God promised, BUT there are too many giants, and they will probably kill us, and the walls are too high and strong around their cities."

Thankfully, two of the spies, Caleb and Joshua, had a different outlook. You might say, they didn't let their "buts" get in the way.

Caleb said, "Let's go and take the land. I know we can do it!" (Numbers 13:30, CEV)

Sadly, the negative report of the 10 spies—the part following the "but"—spread throughout the camp, causing the Israelites to be afraid. They did not want to enter the Promised Land. Because of this, they ended up staying another 37 years in the desert.

So, here's my question to you—have you been allowing too many "buts" to creep into your conversation lately? Are you guilty of being negative?

For example, if your coach asks you, "How's your math class going? I know you were having some challenges." Do you say, "It's going great, BUT I'm pretty sure I'll fail the next test because this chapter is really hard." Or, do you just say, "It's going great! I'm doing so much better. Thanks for asking!"

Or are you allowing "buts" to lead you into gossip? For example, when speaking about your cheer captain, do you say things like: "She seems nice, BUT I heard that she is really fake."

Let me encourage you to use your "buts" wisely. For example, here's a good "but" to include in your everyday conversation. "*But* I trust in you, Lord; I say, *"You are my God"* (Psalm 31:14 NIV).

Bottom line, you should keep your "but" under control in order to have a happier life.

STRENGTH TRAINING: *Watch the way you talk. Let nothing foul or dirty come out of your mouth. Say only what helps, each word a gift* (Ephesians 4:29, MSG).

FIRE UP!: When people think of you, do they think of someone who is positive and uplifting? If not, isn't it time to change that?

MEGAPHONE TO MASTER: "Father, watch over my words and help me say only what Your Word says about me. Help me to resist the urge to be negative, and help me to avoid gossiping about others. I love You, Lord. In the Mighty Name of Your Son, Jesus, Amen."

GIVE A SHOUT!: "I will not speak negatively or gossip about others."

READY. OK: Start taking notice of all the times you say "but" in any given day. In fact, you might ask your best friend to help you get your "but" under control by pointing out each time you say "but" throughout the day.

JUMP INTO ACTION: Memorize this scripture that has a good "but" in it. ☺

"Sin pays off with death. But God's gift is eternal life given by Jesus Christ our Lord." (Romans 6:23 CEV).

FAST FACT:

Did you know that Lawrence Herkimer (the same guy who created the Herkie jump) introduced the pompon?

FIT TIP:

As you work out and develop your cheerleading skills, focus on what you're doing better than you used to, and avoid nitpicking yourself. Remember, it's all about progress, not perfection!

Here's another chant to try with your squad ...

We've Got That Spirit!

We've got that spirit (xx)
Deep down inside (xx)
So bring it up (xx)
Don't let it hide! (xx)
(repeat)

*(x) = pause or clap.

19

Never stop praying.

1 Thessalonians 5:17 NLT

"Pray Every Day"

I recently saw a sign that said, "When life gives you more than you can stand, kneel."

I like that, don't you?

Prayer should be our first instinct, not our last resort because prayer changes things.

You know, as important as prayer is in a Christian's life, you'd think it would be instinctive, but that's not always the case. So, I thought I'd share three "prayer tips" that will help in case your prayer life is not on point.

1) **Pray anywhere, anytime, in your own words.**

Just know that you don't have to be in church or kneeling at the altar in order for God to hear your prayers. You can be sitting at your desk in school, running laps at practice, or lying in bed, and still talk to God. And, you don't need fancy words. Just talk to God like you would a friend.

2) **Don't do all the talking.**

The Bible tells us that His sheep will know His Voice, so when God speaks to you, you'll know it's Him because He's Your shepherd and you're His sheep. You probably won't hear a big, booming voice. Instead, it will be that still, small voice on the inside of you. Not sure if it's Him or not? Well, He will never speak anything that doesn't agree with the Bible, so that is a good way to tell if it's His Voice or not. I find it's helpful to have a prayer journal nearby so I can jot down anything I "hear" Him speaking to me.

3) **Praise Him.**

Always begin your prayers by giving God praise. Don't be like Jimmy who prays, "Hi God, it's me, Jimmy. Gimme. Gimme. Gimme." Now, I'm not saying it's bad to bring your requests to the Lord. In fact, it's scriptural. James 4:2 says that: "we have not, because we ask not."

But don't let requests dominate your prayer life. Instead, take time to thank God for Who He is and all that He has done and is going to do in your life.

Take time to talk to God every day. He can't wait to hear from you ...

STRENGTH TRAINING: *Is anyone among you in trouble? Let them pray. Is anyone happy? Let them sing songs of praise. Is anyone among you sick? Let them call the elders of the church to pray over them and anoint them with oil in the name of the Lord. Watch the way you talk. Let nothing foul or dirty come out of your mouth. Say only what helps, each word a gift* (James 5:13-14, NIV).

FIRE UP!: Do you take time to talk to God every day? If not, why not start today?

MEGAPHONE TO MASTER: "Father, I want to talk to you every day. Help me to find time in my schedule to pray, and help me to hear Your Voice clearly when you speak to my heart. In the Mighty Name of Your Son, Jesus, Amen."

GIVE A SHOUT!: "God is my Shepherd, and I am His sheep. I know His voice."

READY. OK: If you feel uncomfortable praying out loud, or have a hard time concentrating on praying silently, try writing out your prayers to God in your journal. You can also keep track of your prayer requests and praise reports when those requests are answered.

JUMP INTO ACTION: Take time to pray for every member of your cheer team every single day. And, if your coach and school allow it, begin each practice with a quick prayer such as: "God, we ask that You bless our practice and help us to accomplish much today. Keep us safe, Lord, and help us to work as a team. Thank You for loving us. Amen."

FAST FACT:

Did you know that in the 1960s, NFL teams began adding cheerleaders?

FIT TIP:

Always keep some healthy snacks in your cheer bag for those long bus trips to and from away games. For example, pack a banana, a bag full of almonds, and a protein bar.

Here's another chant to try with your squad …

The Cougars Are Hot!

The Cougars are hot!
Sizzle, sizzle, whoo!
The Cougars are hot!

And, we're coming after you!
(point to the other team)
(repeat)

*Put your school's mascot in place of "Cougars."

20

See how very much our Father loves us, for he calls us his children, and that is what we are!

1 John 3:1 NLT

"You are So Awesome!"

*D*o you ever dream of being somebody else? Maybe one of the Varsity cheerleaders who has the prettiest jumps you've ever seen? Or, possibly the uber-talented Taylor Swift? It's fun to daydream about being somebody else, as long as you don't spend too much time dwelling on those thoughts. The Lord doesn't want you to waste your time dreaming of being somebody else because He already thinks you are awesome, and He loves you so much. Think about that a moment—the

Creator of the Universe thinks you are awesome, and
He adores you!

Maybe you feel like you have a big "L" on your fore-
head today. Maybe you feel like you just don't measure up to those around you. Maybe someone has said
something ugly to you, and you keep hearing those
hurtful words over and over again in your head. Well,
I've got news for you. God created you just the way you
are, and He doesn't care if your second toe is longer
than your big toe. He doesn't mind that your fingernail
polish is chipped. And, He's fine with the fact that you
sometimes "frog it" when you do your standing back
handspring.

God loves you—flaws and all. So, quit dreaming
about being somebody else and start celebrating you!
Your Heavenly Father created you, and He doesn't
make mistakes.

Meditate on (think a lot about) verses in the Bible such as Psalm 139:14. Look yourself in the mirror
every single day and say, "I am fearfully and wonderfully made." Say, "God made me, and He doesn't make any
junk." Remember, when you became a Christian, you
were adopted into the Royal Family. That would make
you a Princess! So, start acting like it.

STRENGTH TRAINING: *…and I praise you because
of the wonderful way you created me. Everything you do is
marvelous! Of this I have no doubt* (Psalm 139:14, CEV).

FIRE UP!: When you speak about yourself, do you say good things or bad things? It's time to look yourself in the mirror and say, "Girl, you are looking fine!"

MEGAPHONE TO MASTER: "Lord, help me to love myself the way that You love me.

In the Mighty Name of Your Son, Jesus, Amen."

GIVE A SHOUT!: "God loves me—flaws and all. "I am fearfully and wonderfully made."

READY. OK: Write this in your journal: I am fearfully and wonderfully made. Now, write five things that make you special and different from others. Go ahead … it's OK to brag on yourself a bit.

JUMP INTO ACTION: If you feel less than excited about yourself, chances are, your friends feel the same way about themselves. So, here's your assignment. Compliment each of your friends this week, telling each one why she is so special.

FAST FACT:

Did you know that former President George W. Bush was a cheerleader?

FIT TIP:

It's important to eat something before practice, but any old snack won't do. Try powering up with a nutrition bar or power bar with about 30 grams of carbs and 10 to 20 grams of protein. It's also important to hydrate—opt for water over sugary juices.

Here's another chant to try with your squad …

Stand Up!

Stand up! (xx)
Be proud! (xx)
Say your name! (xx)
Out loud! (xx)
Yell, PANTHERS!
Go, go, go Panthers!
What?
Yell, PANTHERS!
Go, go, go Panthers!
Whoo!
(repeat)

*(x) = pause or clap.

*Put your school's mascot in place of "Panthers."

21

"For God so loved the world that he gave his one and only Son, that whoever believes in him shall not perish but have eternal life."

John 3:16 NIV

"You Belong"

Have you ever looked around the cafeteria at school? Students usually sit with other students in their "groups." While there are various versions of these groups at any given school, you'll usually find the brainiacs, the Preppies, "the bandies" (band members), the burnouts, the skaters, the Barbies and the jocks. Of course, you might fit into more than one of those groups, but if you're a cheerleader that makes you an athlete, so you're probably in "the jock" group. And usually, "the jock" group is also made up of the popular kids.

Admit it. By no power of your own, you have landed in the popular crowd at school, and that's pretty fun, isn't it? Of course, belonging to ANY group is sort of nice. Being a part of a group guarantees you a place to sit at lunch, built-in friendships with people who like the same stuff you like, invitations to parties within the group, etc.

While being a member of "the jock" group is really awesome, it's not as awesome as being a member of another group—the Heaven-bound group. If you've asked Jesus to be the Lord of your life, then you are already in that Heaven-bound group. Whoo hoo! But, if you've never prayed to the Lord and asked Him to forgive you of your sins, then you're not in the Heaven-bound group. Would you like to be? It's real easy. All you have to do is admit that you have sin that separates you from God and that you need the Lord. Ask Him to take over your life. Just pray: "Lord, thank You for sending Your Son, Jesus, to die on the cross for my sins. I ask that you take away all of my sins. I give You my life today. Please help me to fulfill the plans that You have for my life. I love You. Amen."

That's it! You're in! Yay! Find a local church to attend and hook up with that church's youth group. Start reading the Bible and find out all of the cool stuff that belongs to you now that you're a Christian. Membership in this group has great benefits—WAY better than a place to sit at lunch. ☺

STRENGTH TRAINING: *But you belong to God, my dear children. You have already won a victory over those people, because the Spirit who lives in you is greater than the spirit who lives in this world* (1 John 4:4, NLT).

FIRE UP!: Do you ever feel like you don't fit in no matter how hard you try? You're not alone. Everyone feels like that from time to time. One of my favorite quotes from the movie, "What A Girl Wants" happens when Amanda Bynes who plays Daphne Reynolds is trying to learn how to be "proper" so that she can better fit into her newly-discovered father's British political world. She tries to learn to curtsey while in a boat and loses her balance and falls right into the water. Her guy friend, Ian, pulls her out of the lake and helps her dry off. Then he smiles at her and says, "You know what I can't figure out … why are you trying so hard to fit in when you were born to stand out?" Love that!

MEGAPHONE TO MASTER: "God, thank You for sending Your Son, Jesus, to die for my sins so that I could be in the most important group—the group who gets to go to heaven. I love You. Amen."

GIVE A SHOUT!: "I am the daughter of the Most High King. I belong to His Royal Family."

READY. OK: Write this in your journal: I belong to God; therefore, I am valuable, worthy, and loved. If today is the day you made Jesus the Lord of your life, write today's date at the top of your journal entry and write this beside it: "My Spiritual Birthday—yay!"

JUMP INTO ACTION: If you just prayed the "heaven-bound" prayer today, tell someone about it. Let someone know that you are now a Christian. Or, if you're already a Christian, but you have a friend who isn't, why not invite your friend to become a member of the Heaven-bound club?

FAST FACT:

Did you know that many competitive cheer squads require that every cheerleader be able to do a back tuck?

FIT TIP:

The best time to stretch is after you do cardio because your muscles are already warm.

Here's a new cheer to try with your squad …

We're Back!

The Panthers are back.
We're better than before.

So watch out, Tigers—
We're coming back for more!

Striving (x) pushing (x)
rising to the top!
The BEST (clap, clap) you know it!
The Panthers can't be stopped!

*(x) = pause.

*Put your school's mascot in place of "Panthers" and the opposing team's mascot in place of "Tigers."

22

Therefore each of you must put off falsehood and speak truthfully to his neighbor, for we are all members of one body.

Ephesians 4:25 NIV

"Stretching the Truth"

*Y*ou really don't want to practice today. Your muscles are sore. It's hot. You're still tired from last night's practice. The coach is taking this conditioning stuff seriously, and you just can't face another day of running laps and core work. So ... you stretch the truth a bit.

You say, "Coach, I don't feel very well today ... can I be excused from practice?"

"Of course," your coach answers. "Rest up and feel better."

As you stretch out on the bleachers to relax, you smile. You fooled your Cheer Coach, and now you don't have to tumble, jump, cheer, or run today. And, all it took was one little white lie. Ever told one of those little white lies? They seem harmless. After all, they are small. They aren't big, whopper lies. They are little, tiny white lies, and those are OK, right?

WRONG!

A lie is a lie, and they are all sin in God's eyes. Whether they are little white lies or big, whopper lies, they are sin. Each time you tell a lie, it leads to another lie. Before you know it, you'll be telling lies all the time, and no one will be able to trust anything you say. Plus, lying displeases God.

Remember the story of the shepherd boy who cried wolf? He cried for help when he didn't need it, so when he really did need help, no one came to help him. (And the wolf was able to attack and scatter his sheep! Yikes!) Don't be like the boy who cried wolf. Don't get a reputation for telling lies. Be a person of truth—even if it means more jumps and tumbling passes. ☺

STRENGTH TRAINING: *And stop lying to each other. You have given up your old way of life with its habits* (Colossians 3:9, CEV).

FIRE UP!: Do you ever think there is a good time to lie—for instance, if telling the truth would hurt someone's feelings? Is there a way to avoid lying and yet spare that person's feelings?

MEGAPHONE TO MASTER: "Lord, help me to always speak the truth, even when it's difficult to do so. In the Mighty Name of Your Son, Jesus, Amen."

GIVE A SHOUT!: "God is a God of truth, and therefore I want to be just like Him and always tell the truth."

READY. OK: Write this in your journal: "I want to be more like God and that means telling the truth." Now, find three scriptures about telling the truth and write those in your journal. (Helpful hint: You can find those scriptures here: https://www.openbible.info/topics/telling_the_truth.)

JUMP INTO ACTION: Really practice telling the truth instead of telling a little white lie this week. For example, if your best friend asks if you like her new outfit and you really don't, rather than lie, maybe say something like, "It's not my favorite, but you look great in everything."

FAST FACT:

Did you know that many cheerleaders believe that dropping the spirit stick brings bad luck?

FIT TIP:

Sit in a tuck position. Balance with your feet slightly off the floor and your arms in "daggers." Now, lift your legs and arms into the toe touch position. Then, snap back to your starting position as fast as you can. Try to keep your legs straight and your toes pointed. Doing 15 reps a day will help your toe touches improve, both in height and form.

Here's a new chant to try with your squad …

Hey, Hey, Hey!

Hey, hey, hey!
(x)
BNL all the way!
(Repeat—It's an easy one to get the crowd
to say—yay!)

*(x) = pause.

*Put your school's letters in place of "BNL."

23

God and people will like you and consider you a success.

Proverbs 3:4 CEV

"Be the Coach's Favorite!"

*I*f your father were the coach of your competitive cheer team, wouldn't you expect special treatment? Wouldn't you expect him to let you be in the front of every cheer formation? Wouldn't you expect him to choose you as captain of the cheer squad? Of course you would because you'd have favor with the guy in charge.

Well, guess what? You *do* have favor with the Main Guy in Charge—God! The Bible says that He has crowned your head with glory and honor and favor. He loves doing favors for you because He adores you.

You can walk in the favor of God all the time. Here's what you have to do. Start thanking God for His supernatural favor. Every morning before you head off to school, thank God that you have favor with your teachers, your principal, your coaches, your peers, your parents, and anyone else you might encounter. Then, watch your life begin to change for the better. It's amazing, really. Once you start praising God for His supernatural favor, you'll begin to see more of it in your life.

God appreciates that you notice all of the nice things He does for you each day. When you get the last piece of yummy pizza in the lunch line at school, thank God for His favor. When you get to tumble in front of the cheer formation during the first timeout, thank God for His favor. When you forget to do your math homework, and your teacher allows you to turn it in late for full credit, thank God for His favor. Start praying and praising, and enjoy the favor of God today!

STRENGTH TRAINING: *For surely, O Lord, you bless the righteous; you surround them with your favor as with a shield* (Psalm 5:12, NIV).

FIRE UP!: Did you know that one minute of God's favor can totally change your life?

MEGAPHONE TO MASTER: "Lord, thank You for your supernatural favor. Help me to have even more favor in my life. Amen."

GIVE A SHOUT!: "I am highly favored. God has crowned me with His supernatural favor!"

READY. OK: Get out that journal and write some ways that God has shown you favor this week.

JUMP INTO ACTION: Keep track of the many things that God does for you each day. Why not keep a small notebook in your backpack and call it, "My Favor Journal"? Write down everything that God does for you throughout the day. Then, when times are tough, you can look back through that Favor Journal and get encouraged once again.

FAST FACT:

Did you know that All-Star cheerleading is the name used to refer to cheerleading groups created just for competition?

FIT TIP:

How's your pike jump? If it's not too great, try this. Sit on the floor with your legs stretched out in front of you, knees pointed outwards, and the bottom of your feet touching each other. Stretch forward and hold the stretch for 10 seconds. Now rotate your knees to the top and reach toward your toes that are flexed up. Now, stretch forward with your head touching your legs. Next, do the same stretch with your toes pointed. Repeat this cycle of stretches.

Here's a new offense chant to try with your squad
during football season …

T-D!

T-D (xx)
Touchdown! (xx)
(repeat)
(Repeat—It's an easy one to get the crowd
to say—yay!)

24

So be content with who you are, and don't put on airs.
God's strong hand is on you; he'll promote you at the
right time. Live carefree before God;
he is most careful with you.

1 Peter 5:6-7 (MSG)

Who Are You Trying to Please?

*I*t feels great when someone brags on you, doesn't it? Everyone loves to hear, "You look great!" or "You are such a great athlete!" or "You really did a great job tonight!" It's OK to get compliments, as long as you don't need those nice remarks to feel good about yourself. If you are motivated by praise, you'll also be discouraged by negative comments. You shouldn't let positive or negative comments make or break your day.

So, the next time your coach says, "You are the best tumbler on our team," you can smile and say, "Thank you," without getting a big head over it. And, the next time you overhear a cheer parent telling another cheer mom that your jumps are the worst on the team, you won't feel like crying.

Be honest. Do positive and negative comments really mess with your head? If you answered, "yes", you are probably a people pleaser. Ask God to help you let those comments roll off of you—good or bad. He will! Then, the next time someone says something that would normally give you a big ego or hurt your feelings, you won't even notice.

In the world of cheerleading, there will always be people around to celebrate that you finally nailed your double toe touch, as well as people who will gladly tell you how lousy your motions looked in the group cheer. That's simply part of being an athlete. Just remember, you can't let your self-worth be determined by what someone else says to you or about you. Your self-worth depends only on what God says about you, and He thinks you are wonderful!

STRENGTH TRAINING: *Am I now trying to win the approval of men, or of God? Or am I trying to please men? If I were still trying to please men, I would not be a servant of Christ* (Galatians 1:10, NIV).

FIRE UP!: Do you let what others say about you make or break your day? Why?

MEGAPHONE TO MASTER: "Thank You, Lord, for loving me even when I don't perform my best. Amen."

GIVE A SHOUT!: "I am loved by Almighty God on good days and bad days. I won't be moved by praise or negative feedback. I will do my best no matter what and feel good about my performance."

READY. OK: Get out your journal and write the last nice thing someone said about you. Now write the last negative thing someone said about you. OK, now grab a red marker and draw an "X" through both of those statements. By doing this, you are saying, "Hey, I am not moved by positive or negative comments. I feel good about myself no matter what." Now, that feels good, doesn't it? ☺

JUMP INTO ACTION: When someone makes a negative comment about you, follow these steps.

1. Ask yourself, "Is there any truth to what was said?"

2. If there was truth to it, pray to God and ask Him to help you correct it. If there was no truth to what was said, forget about it!

3. Now, let it go. Don't talk about it or even think about it one minute longer.

FAST FACT:

Did you know that more than 50 percent of all cheerleaders also play another sport?

FIT TIP:

V-ups are great for your core! Start by lying flat on your back with your hands overhead. Keep your feet together and your toes pointed at the ceiling. In one swift movement, lift your legs up, keeping them straight while raising your upper body off of the floor as you reach for your toes. Now, slowly lower back into starting position and do this 15 times.

Here's a new chant to try with your squad …

We Want a Win Tonight!

Let's go, (x) Let's fight. (x)
We want a win tonight!
(Repeat)

*(x) = pause.

25

We do this by keeping our eyes on Jesus, the champion who initiates and perfects our faith.

Hebrews 12:20 NLT

"Gone Fishin'"

"*Y*our standing back tuck is so good," Kerry says. "My tuck isn't half as high as yours."

"Are you kidding? You're the best gymnast on the squad," Brittany chimes in.

"No, you're just saying that to be nice," Kerry adds.

"I am totally serious. You are by far the best tumbler!" Brittany encourages.

And, on and on it goes. Kerry is a fisher—a fisher of compliments. And Brittany took the bait—hook, line, and sinker. Do you know someone like Kerry? You know, the kind of person who is always talking bad about herself in hopes that you'll boost her ego? Yuck!

Maybe you're a fisher of compliments. Chances are if you're fishing for compliments, you're too focused on yourself. If you're the center of your world, then God probably isn't. It's time to take your eyes off yourself and get them back on God. If you need the praise of others to feel good about yourself, you're probably pretty empty inside, which means you need a God refill.

See, if we're totally focused on ourselves, then we can't be focused on God and His plans. God has called each one of us to be fishers of men (meaning—we're supposed to lead others to Christ)—not fishers of compliments. So, get your eyes off of you and back onto God. We've got some serious fishing to do. ☺

STRENGTH TRAINING: *"Come, follow me," Jesus said, "and I will make you fishers of men."* (Matthew 4:19, NIV).

FIRE UP!: Are you always fishing for compliments? If so, why?

MEGAPHONE TO MASTER: "Father, I want You to be the center of my world. Help me to take my eyes off me and put them back on You. Amen."

GIVE A SHOUT!: "I am a child of the Most High God, and He thinks I'm wonderful. I don't need to fish for compliments from others."

READY. OK: Grab your journal and draw a big picture of a fish. Now write the names of three people inside that fish. These should be people that you could share Jesus with this week—unsaved friends and family members, etc.

JUMP INTO ACTION: Say something nice to someone today. Maybe you could compliment your coach on her new hairstyle, or possibly compliment your best friend for always being there for you. Say something nice, and leave it at that. Don't expect anything in return.

FAST FACT:

Did you know that Texas is considered the cheerleading capital of the United States?

FIT TIP:

Don't ever skip meals. Being "hangry" is never fun for you or your team. Plus, skipping meals will only make you overeat later. It's best to eat small meals every two to three hours if possible.

Here's a new chant to try with your squad ...

Stomp and Shake It!

Stomp and shake it. (x) Victory, let's take it! (x)
(Repeat)

*(x) = pause.

26

Don't put it off; do it now! Don't rest until you do.

Proverbs 6:4 NLT

"I'll Do It Tomorrow"

*P*rocrastination. No, it's not some terrible disease (even though it kind of sounds like one), but it is a terrible thing. It means we put off stuff that we should be doing today until tomorrow or the next day or the next week or the next year!

Your coach says, "I want you to run three miles a day this summer so that you'll be in shape for competitive cheer season." You say, "No problem, Coach." But, May comes and goes—no running. June comes and goes—no running. July comes and goes—still, no running. And, before you know it, school is back in session, and you haven't even run one mile. Ugh! All summer long, you kept saying, "Run three miles? Yeah ... I'll do it tomorrow." But, when tomorrow came, you put it off another day.

James 4:14 says, we have no promise that tomorrow will ever come, so why do we put off important stuff today? Laziness. Fear of failure. Too busy. Too tired. There are probably a gazillion reasons why we procrastinate, but there is one important reason why we should NOT procrastinate—we might miss out on a God-given opportunity. YIKES!

You see, the Bible tells us that God orders our steps. So, if He has ordered our steps to have us at a certain place at a certain time, we might miss out on something really important by procrastinating. God has little "Divine Appointments" for us all the time. But, we have to be obedient and follow Him—and do what we're supposed to do when we are supposed to do it—to enjoy all of the fun surprises He has for us. So, go forth and do what you know you should do today. God just might have a surprise waiting for you ...

STRENGTH TRAINING: *How do you know what will happen tomorrow? For your life is like the morning fog—it's here a little while, then it's gone* (James 4:14, NIV).

MEGAPHONE TO MASTER: "Lord, I definitely put off stuff until the last minute. Help me to do better so that I don't miss out on anything You have for me. I am excited about my future. I love You. Amen."

FIRE UP!: Do you put off stuff all the time? Why? How does it make you feel?

GIVE A SHOUT!: "I will not procrastinate this week. I will no longer put off what I can accomplish today! Yay!"

READY. OK: Grab your journal and write down two things that you've been putting off doing. Now, write an exact time you will actually do those things beside them.

JUMP INTO ACTION: Is your nickname Polly Procrastinator? If you struggle with putting off things, here are five tips to stop procrastination in its tracks:

1. Convince Yourself: Instead of staring at your homework and whining about having to do it, say things like, "The sooner I get this done, the sooner I can do what I want."

2. Encourage Yourself: If you're putting off doing stuff because you're afraid of failure, say, "God didn't give me a spirit of fear, so I will not be afraid. I can do all things through Christ who gives me strength."

3. Organize Yourself: Make a list of goals you
    want to accomplish by the end of the week.
    Then, check them off one by one as you com-
    plete them! (Tip: Keep that list some place
    where you can see it throughout the week.)

4. Prioritize Yourself: Write down the most im-
    portant things first and work down your list in
    that order.

5. Reward Yourself: When you've finished your
    task for the day, celebrate! Yay for you!

FAST FACT:

*Did you know that cheerleading as a sport is
more than 100 years old?*

FIT TIP:

*Having trouble drinking enough water each day? It's
a great idea to use a buddy system so that you and your
best friend can keep each other accountable in the H20
department. Challenge each other to drink 64 ounces a
day. By decreasing your sugary soda and juice intake,
you're sure to increase your water intake.*

Here's a new chant to try with your squad …

B-E-A-T, Beat The Panthers!

B-E-A-T, Beat (x)
The Panthers!
(repeat)

*(x) = pause.

*Insert your opponent's mascot's name where "The Panthers" is in this chant.

27

If you serve Christ with this attitude, you will please God, and others will approve of you, too.

Romans 14:18 NLT

"OK ... Prove it!"

*I*t seems that everywhere you go you have to prove yourself—in school, with friends, at home, and especially in sports! Do you ever get tired of it? You have to try out for cheerleading every year. Once you make the team, you have to cheer extra hard at the school games so you can possibly be considered for cheer captain. Of course, you have to keep your jumps high and your tumbling passes strong in order to qualify for the All-Star team. It goes on and on and on.

Ever heard the expression, "You can't please all the people all the time"? Well, that's really true. Let's face it. You may not always be able to convince every person of your talent and abilities. Maybe you cheer for a coach who is really hard on you. Maybe your parents are always saying negative things to you. Or, maybe someone at school is always saying bad stuff about you.

Hey, that's OK. I've got good news for you—you've got grace. (No, I don't mean that you're graceful. You can have grace even if you're the biggest klutz in the class.) Grace is unearned and undeserved favor and acceptance, and it only comes from God. You don't have to work at winning His love and affection. He already adores you. He knows you're talented—after all, He created you! And, He believes in you. You don't have to prove a thing! His grace is based on His love, not your performance. So, quit trying to prove yourself and receive God's grace. He loves you, and He wants to prove it!

STRENGTH TRAINING: *For the Lord God is our light and protector. He gives us grace and glory* (Psalm 84:11, NIV).

MEGAPHONE TO MASTER: "Lord, I need Your grace today. Help me to stop trying to gain everyone's acceptance. All I need is You. Thanks for loving me. Amen."

FIRE UP!: Are you always trying to prove yourself? Receive God's grace today!

GIVE A SHOUT!: "I will do my best and feel good about my performance. Even if others are critical of me, I know that I am highly favored by God!"

READY. OK: Grab your journal and write five "I Am" statements in big, bold letters. Use red ink if you're really daring! Let me get you started …

"I am an overcomer through Christ Jesus."

"I am crowned in God's favor and honor."

"I am blessed coming in and blessed going out according to God's Word."

"I am full of joy and strength."

"I am a child of the Most High God!"

OK, now it's your turn. Write some "I am …" statements and read back over them every chance you get. They will encourage you!

JUMP INTO ACTION: If you're feeling pressured to prove yourself all the time, you can bet your friends are, too. If you see one of your friends trying to prove herself, why not encourage her? Tell her: "I think you are doing a great job." Or simply say, "You go, girl!" ☺

FAST FACT:

Did you know that women didn't join cheerleading until 1923?

FIT TIP:

Are you in a munching mood when you get home from practice? If you're like most athletes, you are "Minnie the Muncher" after a tough workout. So, make sure that you have healthy snacks readily available for you. Cut up veggies and keep them in individual baggies or plastic containers in your fridge. That way, when you want them, they are there!

Here's a new chant to try with your squad ...

One, We Are the Cougars!

One, we are the Cougars!
Two, a little bit louder!
Three, we still can't hear you.
Four, more, more, more.
(Repeat)

*Insert your mascot's name for "the Cougars" in this chant.

28

Study this Book of Instruction continually. Meditate on it day and night so you will be sure to obey everything written in it. Only then will you prosper and succeed in all you do.

Joshua 1:8 NLT

"Soak it Up!"

*D*on't you just love to soak in a big bathtub full of bubbles after a long, hard, sweaty practice? Your muscles are sore, and the hot water feels so good. The squishy bubbles tickle your toes, and the fresh, flowery fragrance fills the room. It's one of my most favorite things to do. If I could, I would soak in the tub so long that my entire body would become "pruney." There's just nothing like a bubble bath—it's pure heaven! I just love it! Soaking in a tub full of bubbles makes me feel peaceful and rested.

Do you know what else brings peace and rest? Soaking in God's Word. OK, so you can't literally soak in a tub full of Bibles. But, I'm talking about soaking in a different way. I'm talking about reading God's Word in a way that you are totally into it. When you really think a lot about the Word of God, it will become alive in you.

When you spend time in the Bible, God uses it to change you from the inside out. It replaces stress with peace, despair with hope, anger with compassion, hate with love, worry with faith, and weariness with energy.

Soaking in God's Word every day will keep you balanced and ready to tackle whatever comes your way. You'll begin to bubble over with joy. You'll become a better person—a better student, a better friend, a better daughter, a better sister, a better athlete, and a better Christian. And, you won't even get "pruney" in the process. So, go ahead. Soak it up!

STRENGTH TRAINING: *Oh, how I love your law! I meditate on it all day long* (Psalm 119:97, NIV).

MEGAPHONE TO MASTER: "Father, thank You for Your Word. Help me to love it as much as You do. Amen."

FIRE UP!: Do you spend time in God's Word? Do you really miss reading the Bible if you skip a day?

GIVE A SHOUT!: "I will soak in God's Word today. I believe that it is alive and powerful."

READY. OK: Get out your journal and draw three bubbles. Now write three reasons it's important to read your Bible every single day inside those bubbles.

JUMP INTO ACTION: Memorize three Bible verses this week. C'mon, you can do it! Soak it in!

FAST FACT:

Did you know that the Dallas Cowboys were the first National Football League (NFL) team to have a recognized cheerleading squad? It was in the 1972–73 season.

FIT TIP:

Planks are good for your core, too! Start by getting into a push-up position. Now, bend your elbows and rest your weight on your forearms. You should be in a straight line—no bubble butts! Suck in your belly and hold this position for at least 30 seconds; increase your time as you can.

Here's another chant to try with your squad …

Big G, Little O

Big G, Little O
Go! Go!
(repeat)

29

Do all that you can to live in peace with everyone.

Romans 12:18 NLT

"Friendly Fire"

"I am SO not trying out for the cheer team if SHE is trying out," Macy says, pointing at Angie.

"Oh, c'mon," you urge. "You have to try out. You are so good, and you love to cheer."

Just as Macy stomps off, Angie rushes up to you.

"I am so mad at that Macy," she says. "If Macy is going to try out for cheerleader, I wouldn't even consider trying out. I don't want to be around her at all!"

Yikes! You are totally caught in the middle.

What should you do if your best friends are fighting, and they want you to take sides? Well, go ahead and take sides. Tell them you are siding with God because He is your best buddy, and then offer to pray with each of them. Neither one of them may be too happy with your answer, but that's OK. Your mission here is not to win a popularity contest—it's to be an example of God's love.

Don't become part of the problem by taking sides. Instead, be a peacemaker. No matter how tempted you might be to get involved in the fight, don't go there. Let the love of Jesus flow out of you and over onto your fighting friends. You don't have to be a referee, so put away that black-and-white striped shirt and whistle. Instead, wrap yourself in love, peace, and prayer, and tell your friends that God adores them; however, He isn't crazy about all the fighting. Rest in the fact that He knows the best way to fix their friendship. Your job is just to stay out of it and stay in peace. Peace!

STRENGTH TRAINING: *A friend loves at all times* (Proverbs 17:17, AMP).

MEGAPHONE TO MASTER: "Father, I don't like it when my friends are fighting. Please help me to stay out of it and be the peacemaker of our group. I love You. Amen."

FIRE UP!: Have two of your friends ever been in a fight and dragged you into it? How did that make you feel?

GIVE A SHOUT!: "I will not get involved in strife. I will be a peacemaker."

READY. OK: Grab your journal and write the letters for "Friendship" down the left side of your paper, leaving one row between each letter. Now, next to each letter, write a word that describes a characteristic of a good friend. For instance, for "F" you might write "Fun" or "Fantastic."

If you want, you can send your completed list to your best friend and tell her that you think she is all of those things rolled into one. ☺

JUMP INTO ACTION: Ralph Waldo Emerson once said, "The only way to have a friend is to be one." That's good advice. Try to become friends with someone new today!

FAST FACT:

Did you know that ESPN first broadcast the National High School Cheerleading Competition in 1983?

FIT TIP:

Want to work your backside? Try these. Lie on your stomach and lift one leg as high as you can and return to start position. Repeat with your opposite leg. Your legs should be straight throughout the exercise. Do 15 reps each side.

Here's an offense chant to try with your squad …

Two More!

Two more (x) Two more (xx)
C'mon Panthers, Let's up that score!
(repeat)

*(x) = pause.

*Insert your mascot's name for "Panthers" in this chant.

30

And we know that God causes everything to work together[a] for the good of those who love God and are called according to his purpose for them.

Romans 8:28 NLT

"Down, But Not Out!"

*B*eing an athlete can be dangerous. Whether you are dismounting from a stunt or executing a tumbling pass, injuries happen. Have you ever suffered a sprain or a broken bone during competition? It's no fun. Not only does your injury hurt, but your heart also hurts because you're forced to sit out on all the fun and watch from the sidelines. You want coach to put you in. You really want to compete. You want to help your squad. But you can't because you are on the injured list.

It's frustrating, isn't it? Do you ever get impatient? It's easy to get mad when you're sidelined with an injury. But, getting mad won't get you anywhere. Take that negative energy and use it for something positive. Use it to encourage your fellow cheerleaders. See, you can still be a blessing—even when you're sitting on the sidelines. Maybe you can't be a base or a flyer in all of the mounts right now, but you can support your cheer squad from the sidelines.

You may not be awarded "Most Valuable Cheerleader" for your encouragement from the bleachers, but trust me, your fellow cheerleaders will appreciate your efforts. They need your support. We are all called to encourage one another. We are called to cheer one another on to victory—both on and off the court, field, or mat. You can also use your downtime to pray—pray for the safety of your teammates and wisdom for your coach. Use this time on the bench to rest in God and be a blessing. You'll be off the injured list before you know it!

STRENGTH TRAINING: *And let us not grow weary while doing good, for in due season we shall reap if we do not lose heart. Therefore, as we have opportunity, let us do good to all, especially to those who are of the household of faith* (Galatians 6:9-10, NKJV).

MEGAPHONE TO MASTER: "Lord, help me to encourage those around me, and help me to be a blessing on and off the court. Amen."

FIRE UP!: When you get injured, do you pout or do you use that time to encourage others?

GIVE A SHOUT!: "I will encourage my fellow cheerleaders every chance I get."

READY. OK: Grab your journal and write three things you can do to be a blessing to your team this week. For example, maybe you can volunteer to pray before your games, or maybe you can bake cookies to share at practice. Or maybe you can organize the cheer closet at school.

JUMP INTO ACTION: It's no fun being injured. Even if you're not struggling with an injury right now, there is probably someone on your cheer team who is (or will be before your season is over). Why not encourage that person today? Let her know that she is still an important part of the team. ☺

FAST FACT:

Did you know that there are more than 4 million cheerleaders in 31 countries?

FIT TIP:

It's important to be able to do a tight tuck for both your stunts and gymnastics passes. So, lie on your back and lift your knees into your chest and roll back into a tuck so that your lower back comes off the floor. Repeat 10 to 15 times.

Here's a defense chant to try with your squad …

Take It Away, Big D!

T-A-K-E.
Take it away, Big D!
(repeat)

31

In the same way, let your light shine before others, that they may see your good deeds and glorify your Father in heaven.

Matthew 5:16, NIV

"More Than Ordinary"

*D*o you ever feel like you are too ordinary to do great things? You look at other athletes who are better than you and think: "If I were that talented, I could do great things, too." You work hard, very hard, to become the best cheerleader you can be, yet you're still not as good as some of the others on your squad. In fact, you're just average. You're never put in the front of the competitive cheer routines. You never get "a special part" in the routines. The more you think about it, the more depressed you get. Well, cheer up! Ever see the movie, "Rudy?" If not, you should rent it! Talk about an ordinary guy doing extraordinary things. He didn't have a lot of talent, but he had a whole lot of heart. I've got news for you—God loves to use ordinary people to do extraordinary things. There are so many examples in the Bible!

Look at Mary. She was just a teenager, yet God chose her to give birth to Jesus. How about David? He was the little guy in the family. When his brothers went to war, he had to stay at home and watch over the sheep. Still, God called him to defeat the giant. Amazing, isn't it?

So, cheer up! If you're feeling very ordinary, then you're the perfect person to do extraordinary things—on and off the field, court, or mat. You don't have to be the best. You just have to be available and have a lot of heart. God will take your ordinary and add his "extra," and you'll live an extraordinary life. Be excited!

STRENGTH TRAINING: *For we are God's masterpiece. He has created us anew in Christ Jesus so we can do the good things he planned for us long ago* (Ephesians 2:10, NLT).

MEGAPHONE TO MASTER: "Lord, help me to see myself as You see me—able to do extraordinary things. Amen."

FIRE UP!: Do you feel too ordinary to do extraordinary things? Why?

GIVE A SHOUT!: "I am extraordinary with God!"

READY. OK.: Grab your journal and write a story about an ordinary person doing extraordinary things.

JUMP INTO ACTION: If you've never seen the movie, "Rudy," watch it today. Or, if you've already seen it, why not watch it again? It's a great flick! You might also check out the movie, "Hoosiers." Make it a movie night! Nothing like a great sports movie …

FAST FACT:

Did you know that Johnny Campbell was the first to cheer at a football game in 1898 in Princeton?

FIT TIP:

More core work? Yes, please. Lie on your back and stretch out with your arms overhead. Now, crunch your arms and shoulders forward while bringing up your legs at the same time. You'll end up in a tuck position, balanced on your butt. Next, unfold and return to starting position. Repeat 10 to 15 times.

Here's another offense chant to try with your squad …

S-C-O-R-E Score!

S.
SC.
S-C-O-R-E. Score!
(repeat)

32

Therefore each of you must put off falsehood and speak truthfully to his neighbor, for we are all members of one body.

Ephesians 4:25 NIV

"Cool Today, Not Tomorrow"

From Converse to Nike Sidelines, what's cool in athletic shoes today might be totally out of style by tomorrow. Uniform styles come and go, too. Take competitive cheerleading uniforms, for example. They used to feature longer, pleated skirts and long-sleeved sweaters. Today's cheer outfits are flashier, with cut-out skirts and some belly-baring vests. (Definitely not making dress code at most middle schools!) Basketball

uniforms have changed, too. Basketball shorts used to
be shorter and tighter and cut up on the thighs. Now,
basketball shorts are long and really baggy. Let's face
it. It's almost impossible to keep up with the fashion
and footwear fads in the world of sports. (Unless you're
Serena or Venus Williams, of course!)

Styles change. And, so do our likes and dislikes.
Remember how cute you thought your outfit was the
first day of school two years ago? I bet you wouldn't
even wear it to take out the garbage today. Your tastes
have changed.

Change is just a part of life. From changing fash-
ions to changing sports to changing schools—change
happens. So, in the middle of all this change, isn't it
good to know that God never changes? Malachi 3:6 in
the Bible says, "I the Lord do not change ..."

You can always count on the Lord. He's there
through Chuck Taylor shoes to slip-on Keds to Nike
Sidelines and everything in between. Let Him be the
constant in your life. Run to God when you feel overwhelmed by the changes going on around you. If you'll
stay grounded in Him, you'll always be "heavenly hip"
and ready to face anything—even if those ugly pleated
cheerleading skirts make a comeback! Yikes!

STRENGTH TRAINING: *Jesus Christ is the same
yesterday and today and forever.* (Hebrews 13:8, NIV).

MEGAPHONE TO MASTER: "Thank You, Lord, for being the same yesterday, today, and forever. Amen."

FIRE UP!: Do you follow the fashion trends, or are you a style-maker?

GIVE A SHOUT!: "Styles change. My tastes may change. But my God never changes!"

READY. OK: Grab your journal and design a new sports uniform. Make sure you color it! Use your school colors for fun. Or, design a logo for a Spirit T-shirt that you can sell as a fundraising project. Be creative!

JUMP INTO ACTION: If you aren't able to get new uniforms each year, why not find other ways to update your team's look? You could make matching flip flops to wear to and from the gym. Get fabric in your team's colors and cut the fabric into skinny strips. Now, tie those pieces of fabric onto the flip flops. Make sure they are pretty close together for a fluffier flip flop. Very cute!

FAST FACT:

Did you know that poms were invented in the 1930s?

FIT TIP:

One of the best ways to build strong legs is by running stairs. Not only is this a great way to increase your leg strength, but also it's a great way to get your cardio in—so hit the stairs!

Here's another offense chant to try with your squad …

Down That Floor!

All the way down that
Floor
For
Two!
(clap, clap, clap, clap)
(repeat)

33

Love is not self seeking.

1 Corinthians 13:5 NIV

"Live to Give!"

Ever heard of Esther Kim and Kay Poe? They made national news in 2000—not for their great Tae Kwon Do skills, but for their strong friendship. Esther, then twenty, and Kay, then eighteen, had been best friends and competitors in Tae Kwon Do since they were very young. When the two buddies discovered they would have to fight each other for the last remaining spot on the 2000 U.S. Olympic team, they dreaded the match.

Then the unexpected happened. Kay dislocated her kneecap just before the finals and could hardly stand for the final match—the one against her best friend. Moments before the two friends were supposed to compete, Esther forfeited the fight so that her best friend could claim the final spot on the Olympic team. Esther was simply not willing to compete against her injured friend—even if it meant giving up her own dream. In an act of complete selflessness, Esther gave her best friend the gift of a lifetime—a trip to the Olympics.

In sports, we're taught to go for the win—at all costs. So, Esther's act of selfless love stood out like a bright light in the sometimes dark world of sports. Esther may not have earned a spot on the Olympic team that year, but she gained recognition as a champion of love around the world.

The Bible tells us in First Corinthians Chapter 13 that love is not selfish or self-seeking. Ask God to help you put others' needs above your own. Look for ways to be a better friend. Live the love today!

STRENGTH TRAINING: *Love your neighbor as yourself* (Leviticus 19:18, NIV).

MEGAPHONE TO MASTER: "Lord, help me to live to give, and help me to love my friends and fellow cheerleaders the way You love me. Amen."

FIRE UP!: Have you done any selfless acts of love lately for the members of your cheer team?

GIVE A SHOUT!: "I will live to give!"

READY. OK: Grab your journal and write three ways you can be a better friend.

JUMP INTO ACTION: Do something selfless this week, such as rolling up the practice mats for your coach. Begin living to give.

FAST FACT:

Did you know there are five "Bring it On" cheer movies?

FIT TIP:

Isometric exercises are good ways to train. This wall sit will build and shape your quads and glutes. Sit against a wall, pressing your back flat against it. Your legs should be bent at 90 degrees. Now hold this position. To increase the difficulty level, add a 10-pound weight and hold it out in front of you.

Here's another floor cheer to try with your squad …

Red, White Outstanding!

Red, white outstanding (x)
We've passed the test.
Once more (x), the champions.
Better than the rest.

Cougars (x) oh yes! (xx)
The very best!

*(x) = pause.

*Insert your mascot's name for "Cougars" in this cheer and your school's colors in place of "red" and "white."

34

The words of a fool start fights.

Proverbs 18:6 MSG

"Fight the Urge to Fight!"

"You are such a loser!" your best friend on the cheer team yells.

"I'm not the loser, YOU are!" you scream back at her. "I can't believe I was ever your friend."

Ever been there? Ever been so mad at one of your friends that you screamed ugly, hurtful things at her? It can be especially hard to get along with your teammates because you spend so much time together that you get sick of them, right? And then there's the whole

"I'm better than you are" attitude to deal with at some point during the season. Fights happen.

But, fighting, which is also known as "strife," is a very SERIOUS subject—not to be taken lightly. If you have strife in your life, get it out of there today! Being in constant strife is like inviting the Devil into your home. It's like saying, "Yo Devil. Come on in and make yourself comfy. Oh, and bring all of your evil buddies, like jealousy, fear, bitterness, and unforgiveness with you."

Don't let strife camp out in your life. Fight the urge to fight! When you feel yourself getting mad, ask God to help you control your temper. Instead of yelling at your teammates and friends, stop and pray for them. It's impossible to be mad at someone and pray for that person at the same time. So, kick strife out the door today. You'll be so glad you did.

STRENGTH TRAINING: *Never pay back evil for evil to anyone. Do things in such a way that everyone can see that you are honorable* (Romans 12:17, NIV).

MEGAPHONE TO MASTER: "Lord, help me to walk in love, not strife. Father, help me to be a peacemaker in all of my relationships. I love You, Amen."

FIRE UP!: Is there someone that you need to make up with? Do you allow strife into your life on a regular basis?

GIVE A SHOUT!: "I will kick strife out of my life."

READY. OK: Grab your journal and write the name of the person who makes you the maddest. Now, write the word "love" in big, bold letters, right over the top of that name. That's a reminder that God's love is bigger than your anger toward that person.

JUMP INTO ACTION: JUST SAY NO TO STRIFE!

Following are three ways to make peace with a former friend. If you've been fighting a lot lately, and you want to make up, try these tips.

1. Write your friend a letter, telling her how much you miss her friendship. Make sure you apologize for your mistakes.

2. Give her a friendship photo book. Put together a photo album of treasured times you two have shared, reminding her that you had some really great times together. Then, write a note that says something like, "Here's hoping we can make some more fun memories together."

3. Give her a ringy-dingy—a phone call or a text message. Tell her that you're sorry for fighting and that you want to get together as soon as possible. Then, schedule a fun day at the zoo, the mall, your house, etc.

FAST FACT:

Did you know that the first official stunt, a liberty, was created and taught at cheer camps nationwide in 1976?

FIT TIP:

Squat jumps are good to try with your whole squad. Try some squat jumps across the gym floor, lining up your fellow cheerleaders side-by-side across the sidelines. Bend down and leap as far forward as you can. Be sure that you fully extend your body into a slight curve as you leave the ground. Try to leap as far as you can.

Here's another chant to try with your squad …

Say it Loud!

Say it loud (xx)
Say it proud (xx)
Go Panthers Go!
(repeat)

*(x) = pause or claps.

*Insert your mascot's name for "Panthers" in this chant.

35

I can lie down and sleep soundly because you,
Lord, will keep me safe.

Psalm 4:8 CEV

"Catch Some ZZZZZZZZZs Sleeping Beauty ..."

*D*o you ever have trouble sleeping? You toss, you turn. You roll around and get tangled up in the covers. You stare at the clock. You stare at the ceiling. You try to shut off your mind, but it keeps going and going and going. You need to sleep because you have a big cheer competition tomorrow, but you just can't. The truth is, you're worried about the competition and a gazillion other things. Your mind won't stop. It just keeps worrying about everything. You worry about messing up in the cheer routine. You worry that you won't pass your math test. You worry that the guy you like in sixth period won't ask you to the upcoming school dance. Worry, worry, worry!

Well, guess what? You don't have to worry anymore. You have a promise from the Bible that guarantees you sweet sleep. Proverbs 3:24 says that you *will not* be afraid and that your sleep *will be* sweet. Isn't that good news? No more sleepless nights for you, sister!

So, the next time you start the whole tossing and turning routine, say out loud in your bedroom, "I will not be afraid, and my sleep will be sweet according to Proverbs 3:24." Then, thank God for your sweet sleep and enjoy a good night's rest. "Sweet dreams" is more than just an expression. It's a promise! So, quit worrying and start dreaming about nailing that competitive cheer routine! ☺

STRENGTH TRAINING: *When you lie down, you will not be afraid; when you lie down, your sleep will be sweet* (Proverbs 3:24, NIV).

MEGAPHONE TO MASTER: "Lord, I give all of my worries and concerns to You. I know that You can handle them. Thanks for sweet sleep. Amen."

FIRE UP!: Do you worry a lot at night? Why not just give those worries to God?

GIVE A SHOUT!: "I will sleep peacefully. God promises sweet sleep."

READY. OK: Get out your journal and write five things that worry you on a regular basis. Now, look at those worries ... isn't God bigger than any of those things?

JUMP INTO ACTION: To get to sleep easier, try taking a hot bath right before you go to bed. Lavender bath beads are good to use because lavender is a calming scent. Try using lavender-scented body lotion, too! Also, it's a good idea to shut off all electronics 30 minutes before bed so you can unplug from the world and shut off your mind in preparation for sweet sleep.

FAST FACT:

Did you know that ESPN declared cheerleading was a sport in the late 1990s, giving cheerleading the credibility it needed?

FIT TIP:

Mountain climbers are tough, but they are a good cardio workout, and they also work your shoulders a little. Start in a push-up position and bring one leg forward into a lunge. Then, quickly switch legs. Continue moving your legs in and out quickly.

Here's another chant to try with your squad …

Gotta Go to Fight!

Gotta go to fight!
Gotta fight to win!
Gotta go, fight, win! (x)
(repeat)

*(x) = pause.

36

Delight yourself also in the LORD,
And He shall give you the desires of your heart.

Psalm 37:4 NKJV

"Wishful Thinking"

I wish I had longer legs. I wish I had a stronger body. I wish my hair were naturally curly.

I wish I had a better back handspring. I wish. I wish. I wish.

Does this sound anything like your wish list? Maybe not, but I bet you have a wish list, don't you? It's OK to have a wish list, as long as you're not wishing your life away. If you dwell in the "land of wishing" too long, you'll eventually cross over into the "land of envy." And that's no place for a Christian to live. You see, wishing you had season tickets to Six Flags like your best friend is one thing, but wishing you had *her* season ticket is quite another. So, you need to be careful.

You should be happy with your own life. Sure, there are going to be things you'd like to change, things you'd like to have, and goals you'd like to accomplish. But, you need to be happy with the overall person God made you to be. You need to be happy with the life that you have. Try praising God for the good things in your life instead of wishing you had a better life. Praise Him that He made you unique—with special gifts and talents that He didn't give to anyone else. It's OK to make a little wish, as long as you make a little praise at the same time.

STRENGTH TRAINING: *Now glory be to God! By his mighty power at work within us, he is able to accomplish infinitely more than we would ever dare to ask or hope* (Ephesians 3:20, NLT).

MEGAPHONE TO MASTER: "Lord, help me to quit comparing myself and my life to others, and help me to stop wishing my life away. I praise You for all of the blessings in my life. Amen."

FIRE UP!: Do you spend too much time wishing your life were different? If so, why?

GIVE A SHOUT!: "I am unique, I am blessed. I am thankful."

READY. OK: You know why wishing is so much fun? Because there are no boundaries or limits on your wishes. So, go ahead. Jot down a few of your most bizarre, outrageous wishes in your journal. Describe them in great detail. Have fun with it!

JUMP INTO ACTION: Speaking of wishes, Make-A-Wish Foundation is an organization granting the wishes of children with life-threatening medical conditions. Now those are some wishes worth filling! If you'd like to get involved, go to wish.org.

FAST FACT:

Did you know that All-Star cheer teams began to emerge during the 1980s because some athletes just wanted to compete without school or sports league affiliation?

FIT TIP:

Handstand drills are great because they will improve your cartwheels, round-offs, handsprings, etc. Almost all gymnastics moves rely on good handstand form. Lunge with one foot forward and kick up into a handstand against the wall. Make sure that your hands are directly under your shoulders, with your arms right next to your ears. Keep your core tight and your legs together. Don't forget to point your toes!

Here's another chant to try with your squad …

We Are the STARS!

We are the Stars
From
B-N-L
(clap, clap, clap)
(Repeat)

*Insert your school's mascot for "Stars" and your school's initials for "BNL" in this chant.

37

You're blessed when you've worked up a good appetite for God. He's food and drink in the best meal you'll ever eat.

Matthew 5:6 MSG

"How Hungry Are You?"

When you get home from practice, are you totally starving? After a full day of school and then an all-out, sweaty practice, you might get really, really hungry—so hungry you might even have hunger pains in the pit of your stomach. You've had those before, right? But, have you ever been that hungry spiritually? Have you ever longed for God so much that you really hungered for Him? If you're like most really busy people, you probably don't get very hungry for God or His Word.

Some people think if they read the Bible once a week, they're good to go. But, if the Bible is our spiritual food, we're going to be pretty skinny spiritually speaking if we only feast on the Bible once a week. We need to "eat" of it daily! As Christians, we should literally crave God and His Word. We should think about Him with as much joy as we do a Snickers bar when we're really craving chocolate.

If you're less than hungry for more of God, ask Him to increase your spiritual hunger. Be honest with Him. He already knows anyway. Once you begin spiritually snacking on the Scriptures, you'll find it's a lot like potato chips—it's addictive! That famous slogan for Lay's Chips "Betcha can't eat just one" will soon apply to your Bible study time—"Betcha can't read just one verse." So, go ahead. Dig into God's Word today. It's fat-free and full of good stuff. ☺

STRENGTH TRAINING: *...for he satisfies the thirsty and fills the hungry with good things* (Psalm 107:9, NIV).

MEGAPHONE TO MASTER: "Thank You, Lord, for giving me physical food to feed my body. Please increase my spiritual hunger, Lord, so that I may grow closer to You. Amen."

FIRE UP!: Have you ever been really hungry for God's Word? Do you desire to be closer to Him?"

GIVE A SHOUT!: "I love God's Word. I think about His goodness all the time."

READY. OK: Grab your journal and write your two favorite foods. Now, write your two favorite Bible verses.

JUMP INTO ACTION!: There's no magic pill or potion that will make you crave more of God's Word in your life, but there are a few tips that might help increase your God appetite.

1. GOD TIME: Set aside a few minutes for God each day. Make your Word time a part of your daily routine—just like brushing your teeth.

2. MEDITATE ON THE GOODNESS OF GOD: Ever noticed how you'll desire the things you think about? For instance, if I see a commercial advertising Junior Mints, I'll start wanting them. The more I think about how good a Junior Mint would taste, the more I want to buy a box. Think about God and His goodness throughout the day.

3. TALK IT UP: Talk about God and the new things you're learning about Him with your friends.

4. PRAY FOR HELP: If you haven't already, ask the Lord to increase your spiritual hunger. He wants to help.

5. REWARD YOURSELF: If you keep to a Bible study routine for any length of time, give yourself a little reward. Buy a new bookmark or a cute new journal. Celebrate! If you can keep it up for 14 days, reading your Bible will become a habit. Yay!

FAST FACT:

Did you know that the USASF organized the first Worlds All Star competition in 2004?

FIT TIP:

Here's a favorite stretch of mine: the butterfly stretch. Sit with your knees bent and the bottoms of your feet touching each other. While keeping your back straight, gently press your knees to the ground. You should feel a stretch in your inner thigh. Hold for at least 10 seconds. Don't push until it hurts—only until the point of resistance.

Here's another defense chant to try with your squad …

Let's Hear It!

Panthers (x) let's hear it!
Defense (x)
Get tough!
(Repeat)

*(x) = pause.

*Insert your school's mascot for "Panthers" in this chant.

38

Make the most of every opportunity in these evil days.

Ephesians 5:16 NLT

"1440 Minutes … How Will You Spend Them?"

*D*id you know that there are 1,440 minutes in every day? It's true. That seems like a lot of time when you put it that way, but when you're a student athlete, those 1440 minutes are jam-packed with practices, games, school, homework, and more. It's tough to find even one minute of free time in a whole day, isn't it? That's why you have to guard your time. It may mean saying "no" to some fun things that your friends enjoy, such as spending lots of time in front of the TV or spending hours playing video games. It may even mean saying "no" to parties that happen at the same time as your practices. That's hard to do. It takes discipline and self-control.

Being a successful athlete means being totally committed. Being a successful athlete requires a lot of time in the gym—training and practicing. You can't make the Varsity cheer squad if you don't spend many of those 1440 minutes working toward your goal of becoming the best cheerleader you can be. Professional athletes aren't born—they are made. And, they are made through hard work, sweat, and intense practice. So, if you want to be the best cheerleader you can possibly be, you have to put in the time.

Just make sure you keep everything balanced in your life. Practice is important, but you also need to make time for God, your family, and friends. Ask God to help you use those 1440 minutes exactly as He wants you to use them. When you figure God into your day, He will make the most of all your minutes.

STRENGTH TRAINING: *But seek first his kingdom and his righteousness, and all these things will be given to you as well* (Matthew 6:33, NIV).

MEGAPHONE TO MASTER: "God, help me to make the most of every minute today. Amen."

FIRE UP!: How do you spend your time? Is your life balanced?

GIVE A SHOUT!: "I will use my time wisely."

READY. OK: Grab your journal and draw a picture of your life, showing the things that take up most of your time.

JUMP INTO ACTION!: If you have trouble keeping track of all your practices, games, and assignments, why not get a daily planner? Then, write down your entire schedule. That way, you can better plan your day, week, month, and year.

FAST FACT:

Did you know the most popular sport to cheer for is football?

FIT TIP:

Lunges are a great way to strengthen your legs. A reverse lunge is something you should definitely work into your fitness routine. Start by standing up straight. Lift your right foot off the floor and step backward. Now, bend your left knee to a 90-degree angle while the right knee drops near the floor. Next, contract your thigh muscles and return to the starting position. Now, repeat the same movement on the other side. Alternate for 15 reps each.

Here's another defense chant to try with your squad
when cheering at a football game ...

Come on Defense, Work!

Knock 'em down,
Roll 'em around.
Come on Defense, Work!
(Repeat)

39

... And as the Spirit of the Lord works within us,
we become more and more like him and reflect
his glory even more.

2 Corinthians 3:18 NLT

"Get an Adjustment ... an Attitude Adjustment!"

Many of today's top athletes are turning to chiropractors in order to become even better in their given sports. It's amazing, really. With just one or two small adjustments (he cracks and pops your back and hips), a chiropractor can make a big difference in the way an athlete feels and performs. My daughter, Abby, who cheered all through middle school, high school and even in college, had to see the chiropractor quite often during those intense cheer years.

This has become such a common practice that some professional sports teams keep a chiropractor on call at all times. That way, if something gets "out of whack", the chiropractor is right there to pop an athlete's body back into alignment.

You know, it's the same way with God. He can make just one or two small adjustments to your heart, and you'll have a lot better attitude. With just an adjustment here—getting rid of jealousy—and a tweak there—taking care of that anger—God can totally rework your heart and give you a new start.

Once you're back in alignment, you'll need to go to God for "maintenance work." He will tweak and adjust you as needed so that you'll stay in alignment with His plan for your life. Yay! That's how we stay healthy, spiritually speaking.

So, how is your heart today? Are you in need of an adjustment? Are you out of whack? If so, talk to God about it. He can work wonders on you if you'll let Him. If you're struggling with worry, anger, unforgiveness, or anything else that isn't godly, ask Him to "give you an adjustment." He will! He wants to see you walking in perfect spiritual health. So, go ahead. Get an attitude adjustment today!

STRENGTH TRAINING: *Each of you is now a new person. You are becoming more and more like your Creator, and you will understand him better* (Colossians 3:10, CEV).

FIRE UP!: Be honest—do you have some tweaking that needs to take place in your heart? What's holding you back from getting that much-needed attitude adjustment?

MEGAPHONE TO MASTER: "God, please make any heart adjustments that I might need today. I want to become spiritually healthy. Thank You for caring enough to 'work me over.' I love You. Amen."

GIVE A SHOUT!: Say out loud: "I may be a work in progress, but I am becoming spiritually healthy and whole."

READY. OK: It's journal time. Write down anything that you might be battling today. Be honest. If you're jealous of your best friend because Coach put her in the front row of the competition routine and placed you in the back, write it down. As God begins to "work you over," you'll feel that jealousy and anger go away. When your heart is truly aligned with God and His Word, you'll no longer have those feelings. Once that happens, go back to this page and check off the situations that God has already taken care of.

JUMP INTO ACTION: Think about that person who is bugging you the most right now … your best friend, your coach, your mom? Now, do something nice for that person today. Send that person a card or something. Soon, your heart will follow your actions …

FAST FACT:

Did you know that former President Dwight Eisenhower was a cheerleader?

FIT TIP:

Want to stretch your hammies? Place your arms by your ears and reach for the floor while extending one leg behind you. Return to starting position and switch legs.

Here's a new chant to try with your squad …

PANTHERS ON A MISSION!

Panthers on a mission!
The best in the land!
Panthers on a mission, let's jam!
(clap, clap, clap)
Yell, "Whoo hoo!"
(crowd repeats)
Yell, "Go Blue!"
(crowd repeats)

Yell, "Whoo, hoo! Go Blue, let's jam!"
(clap, clap, clap)
(crowd repeats)
(clap, clap, clap)

*Put your school's mascot in place of "Panthers", and your school's color in place of "blue".

40

Be strong, and let your heart take courage, all you who wait for the LORD!

Psalm 31:24 ESV

"Never Give Up!"

When Chris Klug won the bronze medal in the Giant Slalom event at the 2002 Olympic Games in Salt Lake City, his friends and family celebrated with him. He had not only placed well in the Games but also he had accomplished something no other American had ever done. He had become the first American to compete in the Olympics after having an organ transplant.

Chris had a rare liver disease, one that affects only one person in ten thousand. Because of the disease, Chris needed a new liver and had spent seven years on the waiting list to receive one. One day in July 2000, Chris received a new liver, and five months later, he was back in shape and ready to compete in the sport he loved. But during those seven years of waiting, don't you imagine Chris got tired, discouraged, angry, and sad? He probably knew that many people die every year waiting for organ transplants. Still, he never gave up.

You can't give up, either.

No matter what you're going through, you have to hold on. Whether it's a life-threatening situation or a goal that you truly wish to accomplish—don't give up! If you've been working for several years in hopes of making your school's cheerleading squad and you didn't make it again this year—keep working! I have a friend named Brittany who tried out five years in a row and didn't make it, but on her sixth year—she made the cheer squad! And, she went on to become the captain of the varsity cheer squad at her high school!

Your breakthrough may take seven years to happen—like Chris Klug's. Or, your miracle may be just around the corner. Just know that you will succeed—in God's perfect timing. God knows what you need, and He is never late. You can trust Him. Just don't give up.

STRENGTH TRAINING: *Wait on the Lord; be of good courage, and He shall strengthen your heart; wait, I say, on the Lord!* (Psalm 27:14, NKJV).

MEGAPHONE TO MASTER: "Lord, help me to wait on You. Help me to never give up. I love You, Lord. Amen."

FIRE UP!: Do you have lots of patience? Do you ever get tired of waiting on God? Remember—His timing is always perfect!

GIVE A SHOUT!: "I will wait upon the Lord. I will never give up."

READY. OK: It's journal time. Write the thing you're waiting on God to do in your life right now. Maybe you're waiting on God to fix a friendship that needs fixing in your life. Whatever it is—ask God, believe God, and wait with a good attitude.

JUMP INTO ACTION: Find a Bible promise to encourage you as you wait on the Lord. Here's one of my favorites: *And we know that God causes everything to work together[a] for the good of those who love God and are called according to his purpose for them* (Romans 8:28, NLT).

FAST FACT:

Did you know thatthe National Council for Spirit Safety and Education (NCSSE) was formed to offer safety training for youth, school, All-Star and college cheer coaches in 2003?

FIT TIP:

If you're trying to eat healthier and avoid sugary, empty calories, here's a sweet treat you might like—but it's not good if you're allergic to nuts. However, if you're allergy free, try individual packets of Justin's peanut butter and almond butter. They are all-natural and yummy!

Here's another fun chant to try with your squad …

Hustle!

H-U-S-T-L-E
Hustle for a Victory!
(Repeat)

52302239R00109

Made in the USA
Columbia, SC
01 March 2019